#11 Frances Howard Goldwyn Hollywood
Regional Library
1623 N. Ivar Avenue
Hollywood, CA 90028

MAR 2 5 2002

11

W9-BOO-169

Issues in Focus

Megan's Law
Protection or Privacy

Margie Druss Fodor

364.153
F653

Enslow Publishers, Inc.

40 Industrial Road   PO Box 38
Box 398   Aldershot
Berkeley Heights, NJ 07922   Hants GU12 6BP
USA   UK

http://www.enslow.com

For Ken, With Love

Copyright © 2001 by Margie Druss Fodor

All rights reserved.

No part of this book may be reproduced by any means without the written permission of the publisher.

Library of Congress Cataloging-in-Publication Data

Fodor, Margie Druss.
     Megan's law: protection or privacy / Margie Druss Fodor.
        p. cm. — (Issues in focus)
     Includes bibliographical references and index.
     ISBN 0-7660-1586-6 (hardcover)
     1. Child sexual abuse—United States—Prevention. 2. Sex offenders—United States—Registers. 3. Child molesters—United States—Registers. I. Title. II. Issues in focus (Hillside, N.J.)
     HV6570.2 .F67   2001
     362.7'672'0973—dc21

                                        00-012307
                                           CIP

Printed in the United States of America

10 9 8 7 6 5 4 3 2 1

To Our Readers: We have done our best to make sure all Internet addresses in this book were active and appropriate when we went to press. However, the author and the publisher have no control over and assume no liability for the material available on those Internet sites or on other Web sites they may link to. Any comments or suggestions can be sent by e-mail to comments@enslow.com or to the address on the back cover.

Illustration Credits: AP/World Wide Photos, pp. 77, 82; © Bill Bayer, pp. 26, 58; Corel Corporation, p. 7; courtesy of the office of Rep. Bob Franks, p. 103; courtesy of Rosemarie L. D'Alessandro, pp. 38, 42; courtesy of Senator Peter A. Inverso, p. 81; FBI staff, pp. 44, 90; Margie Druss Fodor, p. 21; photo provided by the Jacob Wetterling Foundation, p. 60; photos by Margie Druss Fodor with permission from Megan's Place Fund Inc., pp. 66, 101, 102, 105; reprinted with permission from The National Center for Missing and Exploited Children, pp. 30, 34.

Cover Illustration: Courtesy of Hamilton Township, New Jersey, Police Department.

Contents

Acknowledgments

So many kind people helped me tell the story of Megan Kanka and other children. First, I would like to thank the Hamilton Township Police Department in New Jersey, specifically Detective Bill Kieffer. He gave hours to offer me insight on what happened the day Megan died.

I am also indebted to Roxanne Lieb of the Washington State Institute for Public Policy for allowing me to use her Megan's Law study. Others deserve tremendous thanks, including Amy Smorodin at The National Center for Missing and Exploited Children for letting me use the organization's resource materials, *U.S. Catholic* for permission to use its perceptive survey, Chuck Davis at the New Jersey State Attorney General's Office for pages of helpful statistics, Paul Bresson and others at the FBI, and to gifted photographer Bill Bayer for his contribution.

My gratitude also goes to Rosemarie D'Alessandro for taking the time to talk about her daughter Joan and her efforts to protect children.

On a personal note, thanks to my family. With much love and importance, I would like to recognize my husband, Ken, for not only reading and critiquing each chapter for me, but also for his unconditional support.

My thoughts are with all the children's families mentioned in this book.

1

A Child's Murder Shocks the Nation and Sparks Change

Seven-year-old Megan Kanka left her Hamilton Township, New Jersey, home on July 29, 1994, to see if her friend, Courtney Foster, wanted to play. Her friend was not available, but before Megan returned home, she stopped and talked with her neighbor about his new puppy. He invited her inside to see his pet. That was the last time anybody saw her alive.[1]

Megan's body was found the next day. Hundreds of people had helped search for

5

her. However, it was the killer himself who led police to the girl's body in a county park.[2]

Megan died at the hands of the neighbor she went to visit, a convicted sex offender named Jesse Timmendequas. She had been raped and strangled to death. Plastic bags were still wrapped over her head when she was found.[3]

Police arrested Timmendequas. Three years later, he was found guilty of murder, then sentenced to death.

This crime shocked not only the suburban Hamilton community, but the nation as well. More than a thousand people attended a vigil in Hamilton to support a law in Megan's memory.[4] Reporters flooded the small community to learn about Megan.

From the murder came Megan's Law, a collection of New Jersey laws passed in 1994 nicknamed after the little girl. President Bill Clinton signed a national version of the law in 1996. The law includes a section that requires neighbors to be told if certain high-risk convicted sex offenders move into their community. Offenders must also register with the police in the town where they will be living.[5]

The law could give other people what the Kankas did not have—knowledge that a convicted sex offender lives in their neighborhood.[6]

Questions, Debate, and Controversy

The law, however, sparked controversy. Each side raised questions in argument for and against the need for registration and notification. Does this law really help protect the children? Do sex offenders have rights, and should they be protected, too? Does Megan's Law help prevent sex offenders from committing crimes? What about justice for the victims and families? Does this law make offenders "serve time" forever outside the prison for a crime for which they have already paid? Inside the court system someone cannot be charged twice for the same crime. This is called double jeopardy and is forbidden by the U.S. Constitution and by many state constitutions.

Do sex offenders who register under Megan's Law face harassment or harm once neighbors find out where they live? In some cases, yes. In Oregon, for example, a child molester was threatened at gunpoint while other offenders experienced name-calling and minor property damage. In two incidents in Washington State, offenders were physically attacked.[7]

These are just some of

President Bill Clinton signed a federal version of Megan's Law in 1996 to help protect communities from child molesters.

the concerns. The answers give many of us a lot to think about. Some people argue that this crime is so awful that the offenders do not have any rights. Others say everyone has rights, including those who kill people.

What made the crime against Megan so memorable to so many people? Maybe what was so scary was that this murder happened in a quiet community that could be practically anywhere—with mowed front lawns and children playing in the street. You could smell summer barbecues and hear televised baseball games through the open doors of neighborhood homes.[8]

Maybe it was Megan's parents, Maureen and Richard Kanka. They led a relentless push for change.

Maybe it was because the horrible crime happened to a child. This put the case in the public eye, sparking dozens of stories in newspapers and on radio and television stations nationwide.

Recent Federal Bureau of Investigation (FBI) statistics show that 760 children age twelve and under were murdered in 1998.[9] That number has gone up and down since 1989, with an average 867 young murder victims every year during that ten-year span. Some children are murdered by strangers or acquaintances, others by people they know— relatives, family friends, or someone else. Hamilton Township's story captured people's attention across the country. Long after the funeral, people were still thinking about Megan.

Grieving Parents Turn into Crusaders

Megan's murder caused a unified roar that brought a community together.[10] Neighbors and others also wanted to do their part to help make sure this did not happen to another child. In just one week, one hundred thousand people in New Jersey signed petitions in favor of a proposed Megan's Law.[11]

While the Kankas could not change what happened to their daughter, they wanted to help protect other children. Parents of other murdered children joined their crusade.

There are other cases where the parents of murdered children tried to make America safer for children. One famous case, for example, focused on six-year-old Adam Walsh, who disappeared in a shopping mall in 1981. About two weeks later, Adam was found dead in a drainage canal more than one hundred miles from his home.[12] His father, John Walsh, became an activist to help find other missing children. He hosts the popular television show *America's Most Wanted*. He also wrote a book about his son's murder and his crusade, called *Tears of Rage*.

The cases surrounding Adam and Megan remind us that children are vulnerable. They tend to be more trusting and to believe the best of people.

Parents typically tell their children not to talk to strangers, but what about neighbors? What about teachers? Family friends? Relatives? When does protecting children go too far? Some say parents can never protect youngsters too much. Others say children should not live in fear that every stranger is a murderer.

In about eight hundred thousand missing children cases in 1998, or 2,200 per day, the disappearance of a child was of such concern that someone notified the police and a report was made to the FBI's National Crime Information Center.[13] This number includes runaways as well as abductions. While the number of missing children cases had dropped from 1997, there are still thousands of children missing. The mission of organizations such as The National Center for Missing and Exploited Children is to find these children and to help prevent them from being abducted, molested, exploited, and victimized.

Faces of Children

The faces of missing children are part of our daily lives. They are on milk cartons, flyers we get in the mail, and even grocery bags. Do the faces ever look familiar? That face could belong to a sister or brother, a friend, or a relative. Even if the face is not familiar, people sometimes read the description of a missing child and wonder if he or she is alive. Behind each photograph there may be a worried and scared relative or friend, desperate for information about the child.

Many of these missing children have been away from their homes for years. With help from computers, the public can see what a child gone at age six might look like at age sixteen. But, police say, the sooner authorities start searching for a missing boy or girl, the better the chances of finding that child. Maybe, they say, the better the chances of finding that child alive. In an instant, a child can be gone from a shopping mall, playing field, home, or neighborhood.

Older children are reported missing, too. Polly Klaas was twelve years old when she was abducted from a slumber party at her mother's Petaluma, California, home.[14] Most people think the home is the safest place; sometimes it is not. Polly was taken from her loved ones and killed.

Murdered children, such as Polly, will not be experiencing family dinners, parties with friends, school dances, pep rallies, proms, spring days, or snowy nights. They will also never get to go to college or spend time with children of their own.

It can take years to find out what happened to certain missing children. Sometimes, we never find out. The National Center for Missing and Exploited Children continually hopes that information about missing children will surface.

An eerie question that many of us hear late at night while relaxing on a couch watching television reminds us of how fragile life can be: "It's 10 P.M., do you know where your children are?" While most people can answer yes, there are thousands of people who do not have an answer.[15]

2

The Birth of Megan's Law

Maureen Kanka cooked dinner for her husband, Richard, and son, Jeremy, then nine, on a night that seemed like many others. Her oldest child, twelve-year-old Jessica, wanted to make pancakes for her younger sister, Megan.[1]

In the early evening of that day, July 29, 1994, Maureen Kanka last saw Megan before going to her bedroom to relax and unwind for a little while. She worked as a dispatcher for a heating and air conditioning business after having spent years as a stay-at-home mom raising her three children.[2]

Between 6:15 P.M. and 6:30 P.M., Megan went across the street to ask her friend, Courtney Foster, if she wanted to play, but Courtney was not home.[3] The little girl was on her way back home when she passed Courtney's next-door neighbor, who lived at 27 Barbara Lee Drive. The man, Jesse Timmendequas, walked up to Megan and asked if she wanted to see his puppy. He explained to Megan that she had to come into the house because he did not want to let the pet out in the yard.[4]

Timmendequas led Megan to his bedroom on the second floor of the two-story house. In that bedroom, a horrifying series of events began. Timmendequas touched Megan inappropriately. The child tried to run out of the bedroom. Timmendequas grabbed a belt off the back of the door and threw it around Megan to hold her back. Timmendequas then raped the child.[5]

Timmendequas worked quickly. He put a green plastic garbage bag over Megan's head, then tied a white plastic shopping bag around her. Megan was still alive, but barely.[6] He put her four-foot-tall body in a heavy plastic spray-painted brown tool box, which was actually a toy chest, and drove his pickup truck for several miles to Mercer County Park. There, he placed her body in a field layered with a thick row of shrubs.

It was not long before Maureen Kanka began searching for her daughter. About 7 P.M., she ran into Timmendequas in the neighborhood. He had recently returned from Mercer County Park.

"I can't find Megan. Have you seen Megan?" she asked him.[7]

Timmendequas said he saw Megan go to neighbor Courtney Foster's house earlier.[8]

The Kankas looked all over their community for Megan. Maybe she was at a friend's house? Maybe out with a relative? Megan was reported missing to the Hamilton Township Police Department at 8:49 P.M. Neighbors and family members continued to help search the area.

The Search for Megan Continued for Hours

Hamilton police brought search dogs to Megan's house to make sure she was not hiding somewhere at home. Detectives Darwin "Bill" Kieffer, III, the lead detective in the case, and Robert O'Dwyer inspected Megan's house.

Hamilton Police Detective Sergeant Charles Stanley, Jr., came up with an idea of doing consent searches. That means a person gives police permission to search for a specific reason. In this case, permission was granted to search every house, car, garage, and freestanding shed on the street.[9] About two dozen homes are on Barbara Lee Drive. The police then conducted a criminal history check of Joseph F. Cifelli, one of the two men who lived with Timmendequas, after anonymous sources told police that Cifelli had a criminal background. Police hoped the check would lead them to a suspect and ultimately to Megan. Later on, police looked into the backgrounds of Timmendequas and the other roommate, Brian R. Jenin.

Cifelli, Detective Kieffer said, gave police officers permission to search his house. What they found made them suspicious. Officer James Nelson noticed a blanket in the washing machine. Police wondered why a winter blanket would be washed in July.[10] Detective O'Dwyer also found a pair of panties with teddy bears on them under the mattress in Cifelli's bedroom. However, the panties seemed too large for a little girl. Cifelli told police they belonged to an ex-girlfriend.[11]

Police read Cifelli his rights. Cifelli, who had a prison record, told officers that he met his other roommates, Timmendequas and Jenin, at the Adult Diagnostic and Treatment Center at Avenel, a New Jersey prison for sex offenders. Cifelli told police he got out of jail first, then Jenin, then Timmendequas. Eventually, after living in a couple of places, Timmendequas and Jenin moved in with Cifelli and his mother on Barbara Lee Drive in Hamilton Township.[12]

Police Learn Criminal Background of Neighbors

The fact that the three men had criminal pasts apparently was not well known. Hamilton police did not know Cifelli was a convicted sex offender until the day Megan was reported missing.[13] Maureen and Richard Kanka were not aware that Timmendequas served six years in prison and was convicted of two sexual attacks on children.

The police intensified their questioning of the three men; their answers were disturbing. During an interview with police, Jenin said that he and Timmendequas were lovers. Detective Kieffer showed a picture of Megan to Jenin, but he said he did not know her. Jenin said he preferred little boys.[14]

Police brought Timmendequas into a first-floor bedroom to talk. Police asked him what he had done that day. His hand shook as he smoked his cigarettes. Timmendequas answered that he was home alone for a short time that day, supporting Jenin's and Cifelli's stories that they were out.[15]

Timmendequas told police he was washing his boat outside when he saw Megan and her little brother by their home across the street. Police decided to take Timmendequas to headquarters to question him further. They felt strongly about him as a suspect. Timmendequas agreed to go, but said he wanted to take his own car.[16]

Police followed Timmendequas to headquarters. During the roughly three-mile drive, Timmendequas had two cigarettes that he smoked and then threw out the window, suggesting to police that he was very nervous.[17]

Timmendequas Questioned About Megan at Headquarters

Once at headquarters, police escorted Timmendequas to an interrogation room where he was asked to handwrite what he did that day. Detective Kieffer would later explain that when people lie, they typically press down harder when writing. When police then turn the paper over, they feel for the high spots to help figure out where the person may have lied. In Timmendequas's case, the paper felt higher in the area where he said he saw Megan go to neighbor Courtney Foster's house. Timmendequas did not tell police anything more at this interview.

Timmendequas was read his rights, called the "Miranda rule," at least four times in a twenty-four-hour period. Miranda informs a person of the right to remain silent (the privilege against self-incrimination), as well as the right to have a lawyer, among other rights. Detective Kieffer said the main reason for repeating Miranda was that any information taken from someone who has not been read his rights could be challenged later in court by a defense team. The defense could argue that a client was unaware he was incriminating himself. Hamilton police wanted to help make sure that details about Megan's disappearance and murder held up in court.

After the interview at police headquarters, Detective Kieffer said Timmendequas gave authorities permission to search his truck. There, they found a key piece of evidence—the spray-painted tool box. The box smelled like cleaning fluid, as if it had been washed out. Detective Kieffer said Timmendequas told police he was washing the boat and spilled ammonia.

Timmendequas kept stressing that Megan was a nice girl. Police let him go home. Two police officers in an undercover car stood watch at his house. It was then 4 A.M. or 5 A.M. after the evening Megan disappeared.

Police called in all their detectives, a dozen, to help work the case, along with New Jersey state police. Meanwhile, neighbors conducted a search for the little girl. Several hundred volunteers, including firefighters, police officers, and neighbors, helped look for Megan. Search teams were set up at a local firehouse.

As the search and investigation continued, an eerie call came into Hamilton police headquarters. A woman, who said she was not psychic but had dreamed about Megan, spoke with one of the detectives and said there was something about a teddy bear and someone named Jesse or Jessica. Detective Kieffer said this was telling for several reasons: Jesse Timmendequas was being questioned as a suspect, Megan was wearing earrings shaped like teddy bears when she was last seen, and the panties found in Cifelli's bedroom also had teddy bears on them.

Police Gather Evidence

Around 8 A.M. on July 30—the morning after Megan disappeared—the police noticed that garbage at Timmendequas's house sat by the curb. In New Jersey, police must have a search warrant or consent from the homeowner to go through that person's garbage. Cifelli, Timmendequas' roommate, gave the consent. Detectives found what appeared to be a pair of aqua-colored, little girl's shorts all torn up.[18] Megan's parents identified the shorts as the pair worn by their daughter when she disappeared.[19]

Cifelli, Jenin, and Timmendequas were then brought to headquarters and put into three separate interrogation rooms. Cifelli handed police receipts to show where he and Jenin were the day Megan was reported missing—grocery and other store receipts as well as cash-machine receipts. Police ruled out Cifelli and Jenin as suspects; they continued to be helpful to police.

Jenin told police that when he came home, he saw Timmendequas coming from his bedroom carrying the tool box. Timmendequas said he was going to get a cup of coffee.[20]

The investigation was now pointing more and more to Timmendequas as the likely suspect in Megan's disappearance. State police gave Timmendequas a polygraph, or lie detector, test. Detective Kieffer said Timmendequas failed the test on virtually every question regarding Megan.

In the end, Detective Kieffer said it was Jenin who encouraged Timmendequas to lead police to Megan's body.

"They got you. They got you. They got you," Jenin said when two New Jersey state police detectives brought him into Timmendequas' interrogation room. "You're going to need a friend on the outside. I'm going to be that friend for you."[21] At last, Detective Kieffer, who was outside the interrogation room, said Timmendequas uttered the truth in front of Jenin and state police: Megan was in Mercer County Park.

Megan's Brutalized Body Found in Park

A caravan of law enforcement officers accompanied Timmendequas to Mercer County Park. One mile into the park, Timmendequas told police to make a right, then directed officers to a wooded area next to a soccer field. Timmendequas pointed to a spot near bushes. Megan's battered body was there, found twenty-four hours after she was murdered. She wore a T-shirt but was naked from the waist down. Plastic bags were still tied around her head.

It was an emotional scene. Law enforcement officers were upset. Even Jenin cried.[22] Detective Kieffer said that this area of the park would normally be busy at the time Megan's body was found, about 6:20 P.M. But that day, oddly enough, it seemed peaceful. Deer grazed off to the right. And soon afterwards, the clouds opened up and rain fell.

Three law enforcement officials drove back to Maureen and Richard Kanka's house to tell them about the fate of their little girl.

Trial Details Gain Nationwide Attention

The trial of Jesse Timmendequas attracted media attention throughout the United States.

On May 5, 1997, Maureen Kanka was the first witness in Timmendequas's capital murder and kidnapping trial in a Trenton, New Jersey, courtroom. A capital murder case means that the defendant, in this

Hamilton Township Police Detective Darwin "Bill" Kieffer III points to the spot where authorities found Megan Kanka's body in Mercer County Park.

case Timmendequas, could face the death penalty. Through tears, Kanka spoke in the courtroom of how she felt when police told her they found her daughter dead.

"I just sat there, couldn't cry, couldn't react," she said to Mercer County Deputy First Assistant Prosecutor Kathryn Flicker. "I was just numb."[23]

The testimony was grisly and even veteran law enforcement officers shed tears in the courtroom. Timmendequas sat at the defense table across the room. His hair was cropped and his white shirt was open.

A police witness testified on May 22, 1997, that Timmendequas told police he "forgot to mention" that he had slapped and raped Megan.[24]

"The tone was very flat and unemotional," Hamilton Police Detective Sergeant Charles Stanley, Jr., testified.[25]

The detective sergeant said that while he was interviewing Timmendequas, the suspect had complained about a bruise to his hand. The injury matched Megan's lower teeth.

The prosecution rested its case that day.

With the police's careful investigation, the prosecution was able to build a strong case. Of the more than two hundred pieces of evidence collected, Detective Kieffer said not one presented during the trial was denied by the court. Evidence included the following, Detective Kieffer explained:

- Rug from Timmendequas's bedroom. The attack on Megan took place in the bedroom.

Megan's hair and blood, as well as her pet dog's hair, were found in the fibers of the rug.

- Screen filters from a washing machine and dryer. Megan's hair and fibers from her clothing were found in the washing machine and dryer. Timmendequas had wrapped Megan's body in a blanket, then washed and dried the blanket. Detective Kieffer said this was probably an attempt to hide the crime by destroying evidence.

- Blanket. The blanket was important evidence because it was used to wrap up Megan after the attack.

- Tool box. Megan's body was placed in the tool box, which was taken from Timmendequas's home to Mercer County Park. Police wanted to take the box into evidence because Timmendequas said he used it to carry Megan from his home. Anything used during the crime would be taken by authorities and examined. Police also wanted the evidence to be available so it could be presented during the trial.

- Decal similar to Megan's clothing found in Timmendequas's home. Police discovered Megan's torn shorts in Timmendequas's garbage with pieces of the decal missing. The remaining decal was found in the dryer. Because the decal is mass manufactured, police could not prove that it belonged to Megan, but it was very similar to the one torn from her shorts.

Detective Kieffer said police sent the majority of evidence collected to the New Jersey state police forensic lab for examination. The FBI conducted

DNA tests for authorities and examined the plastic bags found on Megan, he said.

Defense Pleads Its Case

The day after the prosecution finished presenting its side of the case, the chief defense lawyer, Barbara R. Lependorf, tried to show that a copy of receipts from Timmendequas's housemates showed holes in their alibis. Housemates Jenin and Cifelli gave police receipts to show they were not at home at the time the crime occurred. Lependorf said two of the receipts did not match the time of the murder. She said the roommates could have played a role in a crime, but neither roommate was charged.

Timmendequas's defense lawyers tried to find flaws in the prosecution's case. They also said Timmendequas did not mean to kill Megan and that police had pushed him to confess to the crime.[26]

The defense rested on May 23, 1997, without calling any witnesses. Timmendequas gave up his right to testify on his own behalf.

Guilty of All Charges

After eighteen days of testimony and arguments, a jury on May 30, 1997, took less than five hours to convict Timmendequas, then thirty-six years old, of beating, raping, and strangling Megan. The jury, made up of six men and six women, found Timmendequas guilty of capital murder, two counts of felony murder, kidnapping, and four counts of rape and sodomy.[27]

The next phase of the trial, to decide whether Timmendequas should die by lethal injection or be sentenced to life in prison, was set for June 9, 1997. New Jersey Governor Christine Todd Whitman said she would not oppose an execution, if that was the fate decided for Timmendequas. He worked as a Princeton Township, New Jersey, public works laborer at the time of the arrest.[28]

After the verdict, the defense revealed that Timmendequas offered to plead guilty in exchange for a life sentence. The prosecution said no. They wanted him to receive the death penalty.

Maureen and Richard Kanka were in the courtroom; they sat in on the trial every day. Both were teary as the jury read the verdict.

President Clinton released a statement from the White House about the conviction and the Kanka family's push to help keep other children safe through Megan's Law.

"This has been a terrible tragedy for the Kanka family and their community," the president said. "Megan's family took their pain and helped guide the nation to adopt legislation that is going to protect other children from those who would harm them. We owe the Kanka family not only our sympathy but a debt of gratitude as well."[29]

Timmendequas Sentenced to Death

On June 20, 1997, Timmendequas was sentenced to death by lethal injection. The execution date was set for August 1, 1997, but appeals would delay that from happening. In July 1997, Timmendequas was sentenced to two life terms in case the death penalty was overturned on appeal.

On August 11, 1999, the state supreme court upheld the death penalty for Timmendequas. He remains at the New Jersey State Prison in Trenton, New Jersey, awaiting execution. Timmendequas was still on death row as of August 2000.

While the trial of Timmendequas focused the attention of the nation on sexual predators, the groundwork for the law that would become Megan's legacy began much earlier.

After identifying her daughter's body in July 1994, Maureen Kanka spotted a neighbor gathering signatures on a petition—which was the start of Megan's Law.[30] In a week's time, thousands of New Jersey residents signed petitions in favor of a law that would inform people if a sex offender lived in their neighbor-hood.

Governor Whitman signed the first collection of laws named after the

New Jersey Governor Christine Todd Whitman signed the first law named after Megan Kanka about three months after the child was murdered.

little girl three months after Megan's death. The date was October 31, 1994. The laws were called Megan's Law. A federal version of the law was signed by President Bill Clinton in May 1996.

Many people believe legislation such as Megan's Law helps protect children and families from going through the nightmare that the Kanka family experienced. When President Clinton signed the federal version of the law to help make it easier for residents to get information about sex offenders who may live in their neighborhood, Megan's parents were beside him at the White House, as were parents of other murdered children.

"To understand what this law really means, never forget its name—the name of a seven-year-old girl taken wrongly in the beginning of her life," the president said at that time. "The law that bears a name of one child is now for every child, for every parent and every family."[31]

3

History of Laws Protecting Children Against Child Molesters

Every state has adopted its own version of Megan's Law, so law enforcement agencies across the United States have the authority to notify people about dangerous sex offenders living in their communities.

Laws protecting people against these offenders, however, are not new. Some of the oldest are sex offender registration laws. These laws require that certain high-risk convicted sex offenders give their name and address to local authorities in the communities where they plan to live after prison. California has the nation's oldest law, passed in 1947. A more recent development is community notification laws, which were created in the 1990s. They let authorities tell residents and others in a community that a sex offender has moved into their neighborhood. Washington State adopted the first community notification legislation in 1990.[1]

While what New Jersey did, adopting laws protecting children from sex offenders, was not much different from what some other states did earlier, the story of what happened to Megan Kanka seemed to spark more change.

"It really hit everyone's fears. It was a clear description of what could have been stopped," said Roxanne Lieb, director of the Washington State Institute for Public Policy in Olympia. "Horrible things happen and they grab our attention."[2]

Groundwork for Megan's Law

In 1994, the same year Megan's Law was signed in New Jersey, Congress passed the federal Jacob Wetterling Crimes Against Children and Sexually Violent Offender Registration Act. Wetterling was last seen October 22, 1989, in St. Joseph, Minnesota. He was eleven years old. An unknown person threatened him, his brother, and a friend at gunpoint. Jacob is still missing. The Jacob Wetterling Act requires states to develop registries of offenders convicted of sexually violent crimes or incidents against children. States must also increase registration provisions for very dangerous sex offenders.

The federal version of Megan's Law changed the Wetterling Act in May 1996 by requiring that "the state or any agency authorized by the state shall release relevant information as necessary to protect the public" with regard to a particular sex offender.[3] The federal version of Megan's Law lets each state decide when and how it is appropriate to disclose information about a sex offender in order to protect the public.

States that did not comply with the Jacob Wetterling Act, as well as Megan's Law, faced a reduction of grant funding called the Edward Byrne

Non Family Abduction

Jacob Wetterling

Age Progression by NCMEC 05/26/19

Birth:	02/17/1978
Missing:	10/22/1989
Age Now:	21 yrs
Race:	White
Sex:	Male
Hair:	Brown
Eyes:	Blue
Ht:	5'00"
Wt:	75 lbs

Missing From:
St. Joseph
MN
United States

Jacob's photo is shown age-progressed to 21 years. He was last seen at approximately 9:00 p.m. He was with his brother and another friend when they were threatened at gunpoint by an unknown individual. Jacob has a mole on his left cheek, a mole on his neck and a scar on his knee.

ANYONE HAVING INFORMATION SHOULD CONTACT
The National Center for Missing and Exploited Children
1-800-843-5678 (1-800-THE-LOST) OR
Stearns Co. Sheriff's Office (Minnesota) - Missing Persons Unit - 1-320-259-3700
Or Your Local FBI

Color courtesy of
Tektronix

In 1994, Congress passed the Jacob Wetterling Crimes Against Children and Sexually Violent Offender Registration Act, named after this boy who was abducted at gunpoint in 1989.

Memorial State and Local Law Enforcement Assistance Programs. The grant provides state governments money to help improve the criminal justice system, with an emphasis on violent crime, as well as other law enforcement goals.

While applauded by most child advocates, some of the notification laws have been met with legal challenges. For example, in New Jersey in April 2000, federal courts suspended notifications to review an appeal of the law by the state Public Defender's office; the freeze ended in July 2000. Public defenders have argued that the law is too broad and violates privacy.

How Megan's Law Classifies Sex Offenders

Every state has developed guidelines for notification using a three-tiered approach to decide to whom information should be released. Authorities let people know depending on the risk of the offender. For example:

Tier I (low risk): Information may be shared with other law enforcement agencies and any victim or witness to the offense. This type of offender, for example, could be a teenager who was arrested for having sexual relations with a girlfriend who was under the legal age of consent.

Tier II (moderate risk): Includes the activities listed in Tier I, but schools, child-care centers, family day care providers, businesses, organizations, and community groups may also be notified of an offender's release.

Tier III (high risk): This type is considered to be the most dangerous sexual offender. The risk of committing a similar crime again is high. In addition to the actions in Tiers I and II, members of the public who are likely to encounter the offender are notified.[4] Hamilton Police Detective Darwin "Bill" Kieffer, the lead detective in the Megan Kanka case, said police in New Jersey have to go door-to-door notifying people of sex offenders in their community and keep track of who officers were able to inform. Under certain circumstances, Detective Kieffer said, the method of notification could change on a case-by-case basis.

Megan's Law is not directed solely at people who commit sexual crimes against children, but at all dangerous sex offenders. For example, New Jersey's Megan's Law sets up lifetime supervision of convicted sex offenders. Supervision begins upon the offender's release from prison. New Jersey law also says that no inmate at the state's prison for sex offenders will be eligible for good behavior credit unless the offender participates in a treatment program.

Statistics of Sexual Assaults Against Children

The U.S. Department of Justice released a study in 1990 about crimes against children. As many as 114,600 attempted abductions of children are committed every year by people who are not family members. Annually, there are as many as three hundred kidnappings by non–family members in which the children were gone for long periods of time or were murdered.[5]

An organization called The National Center for Missing and Exploited Children (NCMEC), a private, nonprofit organization established in 1984, works to help find missing children and educate the public about the problem. The NCMEC maintains an updated library of missing children on its Internet site, places missing child kiosks in busy areas such as airports and shopping malls, releases public-service announcements, and mails postcards describing the missing children to private homes. Internet users can tap into a database on current missing children cases, including photographs. Safety and resource information are also available online. The organization has equipment which can age photographs to show what a kidnapped child might look like years after the abduction. This can be especially helpful in trying to locate children who have been missing for a while.

Since the photo distribution system began in October 1985, cards featuring photographs and information about missing children have been mailed to millions of homes throughout the nation. Cards displaying photos and listing information about 3,732 different missing children have been distributed. Of that number, 588 children, a ratio of one in seven, are known to have been found because of this program.[6]

In addition to helping families and parents of missing and exploited children, the NCMEC helps law enforcement investigators and agencies, child-care employees, child protection and social service workers, criminal justice professionals, legal practitioners who work with missing and exploited children and their families, and nonprofit organizations.

How Families Are Reunited

Since 1984, the NCMEC has helped parents and law enforcement officers search for 57,770 children who have disappeared. More than half, or 38,714, were runaway children; 14,941 were abducted by family

Non Family Abduction

 Morgan Nick

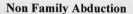 Age Progression by NCMEC 3/30/99

Birth:	9/12/88
Missing:	6/9/95
Age Now:	10 yrs
Race:	White
Sex:	Female
Hair:	Blonde
Eyes:	Blue
Ht:	4'00"
Wt:	55 lbs

Missing From:
Alma
AR
United States

Child's photo is shown age-progressed to 10 years. She was abducted by an unknown white male while she was playing at a ballpark in Alma, Arkansas. She has 5 visible silver caps on her molars. She was last seen wearing a green Girl Scout shirt, blue denim shorts and white tennis shoes.

 NATIONAL CENTER FOR MISSING & EXPLOITED CHILDREN WWW.MISSINGKIDS.COM

ANYONE HAVING INFORMATION SHOULD CONTACT
The National Center for Missing and Exploited Children
1-800-843-5678 (1-800-THE-LOST) OR
Alma Police Department (Arkansas) - 1-501-632-3333
Arkansas State Police - 1-501-783-5195 Or Your Local FBI

Color courtesy of
Tektronix

As seen here in the photographs of Morgan Nick, the National Center for Missing and Exploited Children can make a child look older to show what he or she might look like years after a kidnapping. Someone took Morgan while she was outside catching fireflies.

members; 2,278 were lost, injured, or missing in other ways; and 1,837 were taken by someone who was not a family member.[7]

The NCMEC has received thousands of calls from people who believe they saw a missing child. All leads are checked. They are forwarded to law enforcement agencies investigating the case of each youngster.

The mission of the NCMEC, according to the organization, is to "assist in the location and recovery of missing children and to prevent the abduction, molestation, sexual exploitation, and victimization of children." Specific laws, many of them named after children who were murdered, are also designed to help children and prevent such tragedies from happening again.

Aimee's Law

Gail Willard of Brookhaven, Pennsylvania, mother of a murdered college student, pushed lawmakers to approve legislation that would prevent people such as the man who raped and killed her daughter Aimee from ever getting out of prison again.[8] Aimee, a twenty-two-year-old athlete at George Mason University in Virginia, was abducted from her car on June 20, 1996. Her naked and battered body was found the same day in North Philadelphia. The man accused of the crime, Arthur Bomar, was sentenced to death by lethal injection in October 1998 for the slaying. Bomar was on parole for murdering a man in Nevada at the time he kidnapped and killed Willard.

In May 1999, the United States Senate voted 81–17 in favor of a law named after Aimee that would impose financial penalties on states that had set free violent convicts who then committed related crimes elsewhere.

In a letter to the editor in *The Washington Post* on May 15, 1999, U.S. Representative Matt Salmon (Republican–Arizona) who introduced Aimee's Law, had this to say:

> Aimee's Law would hold a state accountable if it releases a murderer, rapist or child molester and that criminal is later convicted of one of those crimes in a different state. In such cases, federal funds originally headed to the first state would instead go to the second state to pay for the prosecution and incarceration of the repeat predator.[9]

Aimee's Law has been compared to Megan's Law in its ability to help cut crime.

Moms and Legislators Push for Aimee's Law

Soon after Aimee's killer was given the death sentence, her mother said, "Our system lacks real truth in sentencing. Life in prison does not mean life—even life without the possibility of parole isn't absolute." She added that murderers do not deserve a second chance.[10] Aimee's Law, introduced by Representative Salmon as the No Second Chances for Murderers, Rapists or Child Molesters Act, is designed to encourage states to toughen state probation and parole requirements. It does this by requiring a state to be responsible for another state's costs of catching, prosecuting, and imprisoning an accused individual released from the first state. In the case of Aimee, that would mean federal crime money would have to be shifted from Nevada, where Bomar was released, to Pennsylvania.[11]

One of the many people in favor of Aimee's Law was Trina Easterling of Slidell, Louisiana, whose eleven-year-old daughter, Lorin, was kidnapped from her home in 1998 and later murdered. Easterling testified before a House committee hearing on the proposal.[12]

In the *New Orleans Times-Picayune* newspaper, Representative Salmon said, "States should now be on notice that the revolving prison door for sexual predators and murderers must end." Senator Rick Santorum (Republican–Pennsylvania) sponsored the Aimee's Law bill in the Senate. Senator Santorum said tougher sentences need to be handed down to help protect the lives of children.

Joan's Law

Rosemarie D'Alessandro sat in the bedroom of her Hillsdale, New Jersey, home the morning of December 15, 1999, and recalled the events of twenty-six years ago—events that changed her life and that of her family forever. Her eyes filled with tears as she described how her bright seven-year-old daughter, Joan Angela, left her house on Holy Thursday, April 19, 1973, to deliver the last two boxes of Girl Scout cookies to neighbor Joseph McGowan. She never came home.

At first, Rosemarie D'Alessandro thought her daughter might have gone to a friend's house. After calling everybody she could think of, including the police and fire department, she went to McGowan's house and asked him if he had seen her daughter. She said he told her he had not seen her.

"When I went in, he didn't stay near me in the foyer. He went right upstairs. He stayed at the foot of the stairs," she said. "He was so distant, so cold. I left the house knowing I would never see my daughter again, even though I didn't want to believe it. When I left the house and I was walking down the street, I knew it was him."[13]

It *was* McGowan. He sexually assaulted and choked the little girl to death that day. Then, he dumped her body over a cliff into a ravine at Harriman State Park in New York State. The Hillsdale

A smiling Joan Angela D'Alessandro of Hillsdale, New Jersey, showed off her Girl Scout uniform. She was murdered at age seven by a neighbor while delivering cookies for her troop on Holy Thursday, 1973.

Police Department conducted its largest search in the community's history. Three days later, on Easter Sunday, McGowan took a lie detector test and the machine indicated he was not telling the truth when he first denied a crime took place. After speaking with a local priest, McGowan confessed to killing Joan and told authorities where he had put her body.[14]

McGowan was a high school chemistry teacher, someone many people, including the D'Alessandro children, knew and said was nice. He was twenty-six years old at the time of Joan's death.

"He was a teacher who understood children. He lured her," Rosemarie D'Alessandro said during her 1999 interview.

McGowan pleaded guilty to murder the same day his trial was scheduled to start. The trial took place in another county in New Jersey, in Morris County, because of its publicity in Bergen County, where Hillsdale is located. Moving legal proceedings is sought typically when one party feels potential jurors cannot arrive at an objective verdict because of all the media attention surrounding a case. If a judge believes this is indeed true, he or she will agree to have the trial moved to another community where the publicity would not be as intense.

At the sentencing, Judge Morris Malech said, "You have taken the life of an innocent child. All I can give you is life and, therefore, that is your sentence."[15] At the time of the case, New Jersey had not yet allowed for the death penalty. That changed on August 6, 1982, when the death penalty was reinstated in New Jersey. In 1972, The U.S. Supreme

Court suspended the death penalty. This happened in response to a challenge arguing that the death penalty in Georgia and other states was being applied unfairly. A number of death penalty laws were rewritten, then found constitutional by the Supreme Court in 1976. This paved the way for other states to adopt the death penalty.

While Rosemarie D'Alessandro was working to keep McGowan in prison instead of getting released on parole, she heard about the murders of three other New Jersey children: Divina Genao, seven, of Passaic; Amanda Wengert, six, of Manalapan; and Megan Kanka, seven, of Hamilton Township.

"That really stirred me up to say we have to do something to stop this," D'Alessandro said. "I wanted to make something positive about her [Joan's] death and that helped influence me to change the laws."

The law named after the little girl, Joan's Law, does not apply to Joan's killer, but that did not curb D'Alessandro's efforts. She said she is pleased it will help other children.

The law is a package of New Jersey and federal versions that denies parole for child molesters who murder children under fourteen years old during a sexual attack and who are not sentenced to the death penalty. New Jersey Governor Christine Todd Whitman signed the bill in Joan's name into law on April 3, 1997; President Bill Clinton signed a federal version of the bill in October 1998.

In 1999, Rosemarie D'Alessandro still lived at her Florence Street home where Joan grew up, just around the corner from where her daughter died at the home on St. Nicholas Avenue. Two sons, Michael J. and John C., whom she had after Joan died, live with her. She also has two other older children. Although her body has been weakened from a muscular disease called myasthenia gravis, D'Alessandro said she feels more strongly every day that she can maintain her home, be a mom to her children, and continue trying to keep McGowan behind bars.

She began pushing for another law to protect children. It is called the Justice for Victims Law, designed to help make it easier for victims' families to sue convicted murderers for inherited or earned money.

While Michael and John D'Alessandro never met Joan, who would have been their older sister had she lived, they too help their mother send out information on a foundation set up in their sister's name and to fight McGowan's appeals. Michael D'Alessandro was the first child Rosemarie D'Alessandro had after Joan's death. In an odd coincidence, he was brought home from the hospital seven years to the day after Joan died, on April 19, 1980.

"I feel a connection with her because she is my sister. I always felt like I knew her," Michael D'Alessandro said. "I've helped mom. My brother helps, too."[16]

Rosemarie D'Alessandro said she wished there would be no more appeals for McGowan. If Joan's Law applied to her case, he would never be let out on parole. She said she does not want her two sons to have to go through appeals for the rest of their lives.

Rosemarie D'Alessandro (center) with her two sons, John C. (left) and Michael J. (right), who were born after Joan's death.

Families of children murdered since Joan's Law became official might not have to fight appeals.

"I like that the law is making the world a better place. Like isn't strong enough. I like the good I'm doing in her memory," Rosemarie D'Alessandro said. "Inside, that warms my heart and I will continue to do it."[17]

4

Portrait of a Child Molester

When people think of child abusers, they often envision those who take not only the innocence away from children, but also sometimes their lives. That was the case with Megan Kanka, Joan D'Alessandro, Adam Walsh, and Polly Klaas, who were all kidnapped and later murdered.

Molesters are also seen by some people as tragic figures who may have been hurt as children—sexually abused or victimized in other ways.

Experts in human behavior have searched for the reasons that people become pedophiles and child molesters. There is a difference between pedophiles and child molesters, although many people use the words interchangeably. Pedophiles are people, generally age sixteen and older or at least five years older than the child, who have fantasies about, are attracted to, and prefer to have sex with, children who have not yet reached puberty. The child is typically age thirteen or

The current FBI National Crime Information Center 2000 system holds a variety of files, including those on missing persons (with a category for children), sex offender registrations, stolen guns, violent gang and terrorist organizations, and criminal history record information.

younger. Pedophiles are not child molesters unless they act on their desires.[1]

A number of child molesters are pedophiles. However, some adults sexually abuse children because of availability or curiosity, not because they necessarily desire them. While child molesters can be pedophiles and pedophiles can be child molesters, it is important to understand the distinction between the two.

Who Are Child Molesters?

A number of studies have found that many child molesters were abused themselves as children. That seems to be what happened to the men arrested for killing Megan and Polly.

One Web site, for example, features several pages of information on why child abuse happens and the criminal background of those who commit such crimes. For example, physically abused children can suffer from anxiety, aggressive behavior, depression, low self-esteem, violent outbursts, substance abuse, and other problems.

Here are some other facts about sex offenders:

- Statistics show that 97 percent of sexual offenders are males who are, on average, ten years older than their victims.

- Females more often commit sexual crimes in child-care situations, including baby-sitting.

- Abuse by females may be higher than reported because the mistreatment may be confused with regular hygiene or other care.[2]

- A portrait of a typical sex offender can be difficult to draw. Studies reveal that when convicted abusers were asked if they were abused as children, they typically said yes. The abusers also said this is the reason they began to violate others. However, some scientists say people who were abused can also grow up to be disgusted by the idea of abusing anyone else.

Psychologist Philip H. Witt, former director of psychology at the Adult Diagnostic and Treatment Center at Avenel, said problems such as childhood sexual abuse, a dysfunctional family, and substance abuse at home can ultimately lead to abusive conduct. A sexually abused child, he said, can learn that the behavior is permissible.

"But a certain percentage of [abused] kids, perhaps a quarter of them, experience no symptoms," he said. "It depends on how resilient they are, how supportive the family is."[3]

A study by The National Center for Missing and Exploited Children, in cooperation with the Federal Bureau of Investigation, revealed the following: "Although most victims of child sexual abuse do not become offenders, research indicates that many offenders are former victims."[4]

Can abusers be described as primarily homosexual or heterosexual? It is difficult to say. They can be both. For example, Jesse Timmendequas had an adult male lover, yet he molested young girls. While some molesters will display remorse for their crimes, others appear to revel in their horrible acts.

Preferences of Molesters

A majority of studies reveal a higher sexual abuse rate for girls, but boys are also sexually abused. Taking the average of child molestation from eight different surveys, an estimated 70 percent of the victims were girls and 30 percent were boys. Researchers and other experts say boys may be less likely to report the attacks than girls for many reasons, not least because they are taught to be self-reliant and not to complain.[5]

Preferential child molesters, those who have a definite sexual preference for children and are sexually attracted to children, typically prefer boys to girls.[6]

Megan's Killer: Abused Himself?

The childhood of Jesse Timmendequas, the sex offender convicted of murdering Megan, is often described as nightmarish. Timmendequas had a low IQ of 74 when he was a young boy, indicating "borderline retardation," according to John W. Podboy, a California psychologist who testified on behalf of Timmendequas. His mother had an IQ of 73. The near matching score could mean that Timmendequas sustained fetal brain damage, possibly because his mother drank alcohol during her pregnancy, Podboy said.[7]

Timmendequas's lawyers and his brother, Paul, have said their father sexually assaulted both boys and made them watch as he raped a girl. The father, described as an alcoholic, also was said to have killed the boys' pets.[8]

One could argue that the Timmendequas household also harmed Paul Timmendequas. He was sentenced in August 1999 to seven years at the Avenel prison for sex offenders, after pleading guilty to sexually assaulting two girls.

Podboy testified that children who are brutally abused are likely to become abusers. The argument that an abusive childhood gives rise to sexually abnormal behavior was used by Timmendequas's lawyers as part of his defense.

Talking in hypothetical terms about murderers such as Timmendequas, Podboy said such people would be unable to plan the seduction of a small child. People such as Timmendequas are typically impulsive, he argued. They take advantage of a situation when it happens to arise.[9]

The prosecution, however, rebutted the testimony of Timmendequas's abusive childhood.

During Timmendequas's trial, Deputy First Assistant Mercer County Prosecutor Kathryn Flicker attacked defense witness Carol Krych, a forensic social worker. Krych said Timmendequas was an abused child. Flicker got Krych to admit that neighbors and school officials did not observe anything wrong with Timmendequas during his childhood.

Timmendequas's father, who called himself Edward James Howard but was also known as Skip Timmendequas and Charles Hall, has, in published newspaper reports, denied allegations that he abused his son. He was living in California during the time of his son's trial. Timmendequas's mother, Doris Unangst, who lived in Charleston, South Carolina, at the time of the trial, had ten children with seven different men. Timmendequas's lawyer, Roy B. Greenman, said seven of the ten children were removed from the home because of negligence.

"You might have heard the term dysfunctional family," Greenman said to a jury in 1997. "That is a mild understatement that does not begin to describe this family."[10]

Timmendequas Pushes for Life

After Timmendequas was convicted of murder, a jury had to decide whether he should get life in prison or be sentenced to death by lethal injection.

To plead for his life, Timmendequas, then age thirty-six, told a jury (and courtroom) in June 1997 that he was sorry for what happened to his neighbor, Megan.

"I pray for her and her family every day," he said, reading a statement. "I have to live with this and what I've done for the rest of my life. I ask you to let me live so I, someday, I can understand and have an understanding why something like this could happen. Thanks."[11]

His attorney, Greenman, said in his closing argument that Timmendequas "didn't have a chance" for a normal life because of the abuse he suffered as a child. Greenman said Timmendequas should, therefore, serve life in prison.

The jury ultimately chose death for Jesse Timmendequas.

Polly Klaas Is Not Safe in Her Own Bedroom

On the night of October 1, 1993, twelve-year-old Polly Klaas was kidnapped at knife-point from her bedroom during a slumber party in her home in Petaluma, California. Polly's mother, Eve Nichol, and half-sister, Annie, slept in one room while Polly and two friends were in the other room.

A dark-haired, bearded stranger entered Polly's bedroom around 10:30 P.M. The man tied up the two friends in Polly's bedroom, then picked up Polly and carried her out of the home.

Thousands of volunteers joined in the search for the missing girl. Fliers were posted. A banner draped across Main Street in Petaluma said, "Let Polly Go!" The Polly Klaas Foundation was set up. Actress Winona Ryder, who had at one time lived in Petaluma, put up a $200,000 reward for knowledge leading to Polly's safe return home.

All the efforts, unfortunately, did not help Polly. She was murdered the night of her abduction. After a two-month search, Richard Allen Davis, then age thirty-nine, was arrested. Four days later, he admitted to strangling Polly and directed police to her body in bushes along U.S. 101, south of Cloverdale, roughly fifty miles north of Petaluma. Davis was actually pulled over by police the evening of the murder. Sheriff's deputies responded to a report of a trespasser in Sonoma County and found Davis, but they did not know that Polly had been kidnapped. The deputies ended up helping Davis remove his car from a ditch and get back on the road. Some think that, had more information about his criminal past been available to the officers, Polly may have survived. Others speculate that he had already killed her.

Davis was sentenced to death for Polly's murder. Unlike Timmendequas, who was contrite at times in the courtroom, Davis seemed just the opposite. Photographs in the media showed Davis appearing to smirk. He looked as if he were almost smiling in a menacing way in the courtroom. Years earlier, in 1977, when asked by a judge if he felt remorse for his violence, Davis had said: "If I did, I wouldn't have done it."[12] But that was not the worst of it.

Polly's Murderer Sentenced

At his sentencing on September 26, 1996, Davis defiantly said it was Polly's father who had actually molested her, and that Polly had pleaded, "Don't do me like my dad." The courtroom erupted.

San Jose City Attorney Mike Groves, a close friend of Polly's father, Marc Klaas, shouted: "Burn in hell, Davis."[13] Polly's father lunged toward Davis, but deputies escorted him from the courtroom.

Davis's comments outraged many people across the country.

"Here's a guy who should be begging for mercy and he has the gall to make up this statement," said John Walsh, father of six-year-old murder victim Adam Walsh and host of the television show *America's Most Wanted*. "That was directed to break Marc Klaas's heart."[14]

Judge Thomas C. Hastings told Davis, then

forty-two, that "his conduct" made his difficult decision "very easy today."[15] Hastings sentenced Davis to death. He also received life in prison for kidnapping and committing an obscene act on a child, as well as an additional thirty-one years for other crimes relating to the night he kidnapped and strangled Polly.

Marc Klaas addressed the court during the sentencing and said to Davis: "Mr. Davis, when you get to where you're going, say hello to Hitler, say hello to [Jeffrey] Dahmer and say hello to [Ted] Bundy."[16]

Convicted serial murderers, Bundy was executed in 1989 and Dahmer was killed in prison by another inmate in 1994.

Davis is on death row at the San Quentin State Prison in San Quentin, California.

Who Was Polly's Killer?

While Davis's behavior differed in the courtroom from that of Timmendequas, their childhoods were similar in their violence. Davis's childhood mimics that of many violent criminals. He reportedly grew up in a home with little love and a lot of violence. Born in 1954 in San Francisco, he was one of five children. His younger sister, Darlene Schwarm, said in a May 1996 issue of *People* magazine that she remembered a mixed-up and dangerous childhood.

Her father, Robert Davis, a truck driver and longshoreman, threw Richard against the wall when he was a young boy and later broke his jaw. If their mother, Evelyn Davis, caught Richard or his two brothers smoking or lying, Schwarm said, "She held their hands over the gas stove burner until they got blisters on them."

Young Richard Davis was known to pour gasoline on cats and set them on fire. He started his criminal behavior before he was a teenager. By the time he was twelve, he was burglarizing homes and stealing from mailboxes.[17]

Davis later told a psychiatrist he began hearing voices in his head after the apparent suicide of his girlfriend, Marlene Voris. A psychiatrist who spoke with Davis in 1977, Dr. George Ponomareff, said: "He describes a number of instances of his responding to this voice with criminal behavior."[18]

While nobody is certain why Davis picked Polly, he has said he was under the influence of drugs and alcohol at the time of the kidnapping. He also said he chose the Klaas home at random.

Adam Walsh: America's Most Wanted

Like Davis, Ottis Toole, the suspected killer of six-year-old Adam Walsh, who was abducted from the toy department of a Sears store in a Florida shopping mall in 1981, also appeared to show little or no regret for his crime.

Toole, who confessed to murdering Adam and later denied it, said that, for him, killing was "like smoking a cigarette."[19] In 1996, though, while in prison, he said he felt badly about killing the little boy, according to a newspaper report.[20]

What happened at the Sears store on July 27,

1981, can be described as every parent's nightmare. Many children are drawn to toys while shopping with their parents. Adam was no different. His mother, Reve Walsh, told Adam that he could go to the Sears toy department while she was in the store's lamp section. Reve Walsh was gone for a few minutes, but that gave someone enough time to lure Adam from the store and into a car. The suspect, Toole, told police that once Adam was in the car, he locked the windows using the driver's side control. Toole said he hit Adam when the little boy started crying. Adam was knocked unconscious and it was then that Toole, fearing he could be identified, decapitated the boy with a bayonet.[21] A bayonet is a blade that can be attached to a rifle.

Meanwhile, Reve Walsh searched for Adam at the mall. "It was like one of those horror movies," she said.[22]

Community Searches for Adam

Reve and John Walsh knew their son had not just taken off.

Walsh told himself:

> If he's not out wandering around, or trying to find his way home, and he hasn't fallen into a canal, then maybe a woman who recently had a miscarriage, or someone who had lost a child hit by a car, or a set of grandparents whose little grandson has been tragically killed in an accident, someone like that must have him. And they're going to bring him back, because they're loving people.[23]

The community came together and many people

joined in the search for Adam. Posters offering a $5,000 reward for Adam's safe return were circulated. Delta and Eastern Airlines gave the posters to airports across the country. The posters featured a photograph of a smiling Adam, wearing a red baseball cap over his blond hair, taken just a week before the abduction. The Florida Game and Fresh Water Fish Commission donated a helicopter and the time of wildlife officers to help look for Adam. Burger King helped feed searchers by donating ham and cheese sandwiches and gallons of orange drink.

Phone tips came in to police. People thought they spotted Adam. Psychics called with tips. One said Adam was frightened, but all right. But Adam was already dead when this massive search was underway. He was killed soon after he was taken from the Hollywood, Florida, mall.

Adam Is Found

Two weeks after he was reported missing, fishermen noticed what looked like a doll's head floating in a drainage canal near Florida's Turnpike. The head turned out to be Adam's.

Toole, described as a sociopath with a low IQ, wrote a horrific letter to John Walsh while in jail:

Dear Walsh,

You know the story but you don't know where his bones are.

Here's my deal. You pay me money and I'll tell you where the bones are so you can get them buried all decent and Christian.

I get $5,OOO as "good faith" money. Then when
I show you some bones I get $45,OOO. You get
a lawyer to make up a paper like that.

I remember how the little [expletive] was crying
for his mommy. . . . Now you want his bones
or not?

Sincerely,

Ottis E. Toole[24]

Toole was under arrest for a fatal arson case when
he reportedly confessed to abducting Adam. Though
he was a top suspect in Adam's killing, he was not
charged with the murder. Police had said Toole would
be charged in the crime, but he was not indicted. John
Walsh said that perhaps authorities thought: Toole is
in prison, anyway. What's the difference?[25]

In 1996, Toole died of cirrhosis of the liver in
prison, where he was serving several life sentences for
unrelated crimes.

The death of Adam Walsh was just the beginning
of a crusade by his father not only to help families of
missing children, but also to bring justice to unsolved
crimes. John Walsh went on to host the popular
television program *America's Most Wanted*, which
features information about wanted fugitives in the
hopes of tracking them down. The television program
has directly helped lead to the capture of 621
dangerous criminals as of August 2OOO. Twenty-eight
missing and/or kidnapped children have been found
alive as a result of the television program. Walsh also
cofounded The National Center for Missing and
Exploited Children.

5

The Case for Megan's Law: Protection

One of the strongest supporters of Megan's Law is Megan Kanka's mother, Maureen, who still lives in the Hamilton Township, New Jersey, home where she raised her daughter and her other children.

"If we had known there was a pedophile living on our street, my daughter would be alive today," Kanka said in September 1994 while pushing to get the bill named after her daughter approved by lawmakers in New Jersey.[1]

Both Maureen and her husband, Richard, attended the ceremony about a month later when New Jersey Governor Christine Todd Whitman signed laws stating that sex offenders must register with police departments after their release and that authorities need to notify neighbors when certain high-risk offenders move to a community.

At the signing, Governor Whitman said: "This legislation breaks new ground in public protection, especially in the area of notification."[2]

Other parents of murdered children also attended the bill signing. Maureen Kanka seemed particularly moved by the ceremony.

Before Megan's killer was sentenced to die by lethal injection, New Jersey Governor Christine Todd Whitman said she would not oppose the death penalty in this case.

"This is a very emotional day for us, but we are very pleased," Kanka said at the time. "To say thank you is a very hollow word. We can't begin to show how much appreciation we have for everybody that is out there."[3]

The Idea for a Law Protecting Children

The push for Megan's Law began in suburban Hamilton Township after seven-year-old Megan was raped and murdered by twice-convicted child molester Jesse Timmedequas, a neighbor. The same day that the Kankas identified the body of their little girl, neighbors began gathering signatures on a petition. It said people, by law, should be notified if a sex offender lives in their community.

News of Megan's Law in New Jersey quickly reached a national level. Less than two years after Governor Whitman signed Megan's Law, President Bill Clinton signed a federal version of the law on May 17, 1996. The president has said that sex offender registration, part of the Jacob Wetterling Crimes Against Children and Sexually Violent Offender Registration Act, can greatly help in the investigation of sex crimes. He also said that studies have shown that sex offenders often repeat their crimes.

"Today, America circles the wagon around our children. Megan's Law will protect tens of millions of families from the dread of what they do not know. It will give more peace of mind to our parents," he said just before signing the bill into law.[4]

The president then thanked Congress for passing Megan's Law, those who fought for the bill, and the families of murdered and missing children.

Megan's murder and the legislation named after her continued to make headlines years after the young girl's death. Protecting children often brings out passionate statements from many people, including parents, politicians, homeowners, and many others. For example, while serving as New York State attorney general, Dennis C. Vacco, who like many officials had come out in favor of notification laws, released a statement to the media in 1998.

"Somewhere in New York tonight, a mother or father will tuck a child into bed knowing that he or she is a little safer from sexual predators thanks to 'Megan's Law,'" he said. "Since the statute went on the books in New York in January 1996, more than six thousand convicted sexual offenders have been required to register their names and addresses with law enforcement agencies."[5]

The former attorney general has said that the

A foundation set up in the name of Jacob Wetterling of Minnesota was created to focus national attention on missing children.

registration of sex offenders gives police another tool to investigate sex crimes. He added that someday people will be able to go into their local police station and ask for the list of sexual predators in their zip code. California already has such a system with help from a CD–ROM and other electronic media. However, Vacco cautioned that parents cannot look to Megan's Law as a cure-all for problems with sex offenders:

> Megan's Law is certainly not a panacea, and parents need to be vigilant in monitoring their children's activities and providing appropriate counseling regarding the dangers that lurk in our open society. The challenge before us now is to build upon Megan's Law and thus fortify the protection that it offers.[6]

Others also have said the law has flaws. Megan's mother said that while the law named after her daughter was not "foolproof," it would help parents warn their children about sex offenders in their communities.[7]

Megan's Law Described as a Milestone

In *A Report to The Nation* from The National Center for Missing and Exploited Children, and such law enforcement agencies as the Office of Juvenile Justice and Delinquency Prevention, the passage of Megan's Law and the Jacob Wetterling Crimes Against Children and Sexually Violent Offender Registration Act were listed as milestones for missing and exploited children. The report says that law enforcement organizations contend that laws such as Megan's Law help them protect the public.

President Clinton also voiced his support of registration systems and how they can help authorities investigate sex crimes. He said that state-based registration systems let law enforcement agencies "communicate with each other" about sex offenders who cross state lines.

"When sex offenders move, the law should move with them," the president said in a memorandum to the attorney general.[8]

Once police learn about an offender who moves into a community, law enforcement officers can monitor the situation and be alert for anything that may be a problem. This can include a child molester who has gotten a job at a school or a day care center—which could lead to a tempting situation for a sex offender.

"Additionally, the community may aid police in preventing crimes by exercising greater attention and caution with regard to sex offenders living among them. Police cannot patrol every neighborhood every moment, and many parents often mistake a child molester's attentions as an innocent love of children. Such a combination has resulted in more than one tragic situation," according to the NCMEC's *A Report to the Nation*.[9]

The report urged every state to enact Megan's Law.

Some states, such as Florida, have an online registry that can be reviewed on the World Wide Web.

Law Enforcement Officials and Megan's Law

Hamilton Township Detective Kieffer said that Megan's Law can help law enforcement officials in many ways. The law lets police learn more easily the background of offenders who live in their town. Also, in New Jersey, convicted sex offenders have to give blood for DNA profiling.

New Jersey authorities keep the results of more than five thousand DNA samples on file. The genetic "fingerprints" can help solve future sex crimes because blood from a scene can be compared to the DNA data. DNA information could ultimately help police find the person suspected of the crime. Critics have argued that DNA databases can violate a person's privacy rights. They are especially concerned that New Jersey and other states are considering whether to expand their DNA files to include other criminals besides convicted sex offenders. DNA cannot only detail a person's medical history and illnesses, but it can also offer information about that person's blood relatives.

"Sadly, New Jersey is simply falling in the footsteps of most other states," said Barry Steinhardt, associate director of the American Civil Liberties Union.[10]

State Attorney General John J. Farmer highlighted the benefits of DNA sampling: "The kind of database we're establishing will allow us in the future to solve a lot of crimes we would not have in the past."

Farmer added that DNA will only be used for law enforcement purposes, such as identifying suspects.[11]

Other types of databases can help police officers keep a watchful eye on the communities they protect. For example, Detective Kieffer started a filing system of sex offenders living in Hamilton Township. Next to the name, he lists the type of car he or she drives, why the person was convicted, sexual preference, and other information. This information can be especially helpful if police are looking for a suspect with a specific background.

Enormous Support Revealed for Megan's Law

While support for Megan's Law was generally widespread among the public, many had reservations about specific parts of the legislation.

About two weeks before Governor Whitman signed Megan's Law, *The* (Bergen) *Record* conducted a telephone poll of 1,066 New Jersey residents age eighteen and older. The survey revealed that many people in the state supported the notification law. However, concerns were expressed about the section of the law that says they will be informed only of high-risk offenders. They hoped for more notification. While 90 percent of the people polled favored the legislation named after Megan, 83 percent said neighbors should be told when a sex offender moves into the community.[12]

In 1998, Governor Whitman hailed a U.S. Supreme Court decision not to hear an appeal of Megan's Law brought by the Public Defender's office on behalf of sex offenders. While the action can never erase the tragedy of Megan's death, the governor said she was hopeful that the decision would bring some comfort to the Kanka family and security to neighborhoods.[13]

"New Jersey has already been implementing Megan's Law because we believe that it is our right and obligation to provide every protection for communities from potentially dangerous sex offenders," Governor Whitman said. "We will continue to do so."[14]

Survey Shows Mixed Feelings on Handling of Molesters

In a survey of subscribers to a national magazine, readers clearly expressed a strong desire that sex offenders be dealt with in a way that could keep them from repeating their crimes. Men and women from all over the United States offered suggestions on ways to do that.

When asked the best way for the legal system to deal with convicted child molesters who are released from prison, responses ranged from requiring ongoing counseling after release to mandating that all child molesters register with the local police department. Some respondents also said child molesters should not be released into society, while others suggested they be placed in halfway houses. Rehabilitation, a reader said, is the best solution—if the resources and personnel are available.

Readers also said convicted child molesters should not be allowed to work or volunteer in jobs that involve contact with persons under the age of twenty-one. Information about their criminal records should be made available to employers and landlords.

When asked what they would do if they knew a convicted child molester lived in their neighborhood, some parents said they would warn their children to stay away from the molester. Others said they would organize a campaign to force the molester out of the neighborhood while another respondent said it is important to be aware, but treat a past offender fairly.

In the case of Megan's Law, 67 percent of those surveyed agreed that the public good outweighs the right to privacy, while 26 percent of the respondents disagreed.[15] This poll, similar to the one conducted by *The* (Bergen) *Record*, revealed that more people seemed to support the law than oppose it.

Megan's Law has fueled tremendous discussion. Many people say the benefits of the law are more important than the privacy of offenders.

In the year 2001, the Kanka family still lived across the street from the spot where their daughter Megan was murdered. Their front porch featured a clear view of the park named after Megan.

Others argue that the law causes a number of concerns because it can lead, not only to privacy violations, but also to vigilantism (citizens taking the law into their own hands) and the treating of the offender as an outcast.

The National Center for Missing and Exploited Children, which supports sex-offender registration and community notification, said that states "should adopt a policy of zero tolerance regarding acts of harassment or vigilante violence directed at offenders."[16] The organization also said that a community should be educated and prepared for a sex offender's release through forums and public-education programs.

6

The Case Against Megan's Law: Privacy Violation

Years after the signing of the first Megan's Law in New Jersey to help protect children against sexual predators, the specifics of the legislation continue to be challenged. Government officials, offenders, and others criticize the law. They say notifying the community of an offender's past violates that person's privacy, can drive the person from his or her home, and keeps him from getting on with his life.

While numerous people favor Megan's Law, some wonder why a man or woman who served time for a crime has to continue paying for that crime by letting a community know his or her past. Others say notification takes away from the efforts to rehabilitate sex offenders, which they see as a more humane and constitutional way of dealing with the problem.

Since its passage, Megan's Law has been challenged in various ways. In general, the courts have upheld the notification process.

In one of the more recent actions, Judge Maryanne Trump Barry of the 3rd U.S. Circuit Court of Appeals in Philadelphia, Pennsylvania, lifted a freeze on Megan's Law notifications, then later backed new, tougher notification guidelines.

In July 2000, Barry said states can once again warn neighbors when a sex offender has moved into their community.[1] The ruling was in response to an April 2000 suspension by a lower court of notifications in New Jersey. Federal district court judges said they wanted to review an appeal by the state's Public Defender's office, which argued that the law is too far-reaching. That was the second time the court had stopped notifications in the state.

Four months before the suspension, a federal judge said the notification part of Megan's Law should be overhauled. U.S. District Judge Joseph E. Irenas in Camden, New Jersey, ordered the state of New Jersey to come up with new ways to prevent leaks of data about sex offenders. The judge highlighted a case in which the home address of a high-risk offender and a map leading there was published in a Middlesex County, New Jersey, newspaper. The information about the offender was distributed to more people than originally intended.

"It is a difficult proposition to place confidential information in the hands of the public and then require them to keep it private, especially information which may have an effect on the safety and well-being of the community," Irenas said in his ruling.[2]

Several months later, Irenas accepted proposed new state regulations that said people notified under Megan's Law need to sign their names and agree not to let anyone unauthorized know about a sex offender living nearby. Those not allowed to know include friends and neighbors living outside the notification area. Someone who refuses to sign could not get the offender's home address. However, that person would be able to get the street or apartment building where the offender lived. Barry supported the lower court's approval of the updated regulations.

New Jersey Assistant Deputy Public Defender Ed Barocas said the information was still an invasion of privacy because residents could find out an exact address on their own.[3] The Public Defender's office in New Jersey, which has represented sex offenders in court, has also complained that confidentiality rules were being ignored.

"The safeguards aren't appropriate," said Jeff Beach, a Public Defender's office spokesman. "The mix of cases that we presented all had evidence of further dissemination, such as copies of notices being put up on telephone poles. Some also did include such things as anonymous letters being sent to [sex offenders] . . . that said, in effect, 'We're watching you.'"[4]

Does Notification Prevent Sex Offenders From Getting on With Their Lives?

Elisabeth Semel of the National Association of Criminal Defense Lawyers has said, "Notification makes it virtually impossible for these guys to start a new life. Don't they deserve a second chance?"[5]

A January 31, 2000, editorial in *The* (Bergen) *Record* contended that "the state would be wise to improve its system for notifying communities about the presence of sex offenders. To be effective, the law must be fair."

The editorial highlighted a procedural change proposed by the state Office of the Public Defender, which would require that people notified of the presence of a sex offender have to sign a form saying they would follow the law's intent.

"At the very least, the form would serve as a deterrent—a clear reminder that improperly disseminating [that is, distributing] this information is against the law," the editorial said.

Assistant Deputy Public Defender Barocas said people who give out information on sex offenders to those out of the notification range should face criminal contempt charges.[6] The information can include putting up signs or contacting the media.

In 1999, Matthew Muraskin, attorney in chief for the Legal Aid Society of Nassau County, Long Island, New York, said Megan's Law "caters to our vindictive nature."[7] He said that he opposes all kinds of notification laws.

"If your identity is known, you become a

hounded individual. If you're driven out of one neighborhood, you'll end up in another neighborhood," he said. If people do their time, he said, that should be enough.[8]

This could be the scenario of all neighborhoods where sex offenders live—they might constantly be forced from one community to the next.

Identity of Molesters Can Lead to Vigilantism

After people serve time in prison for a crime, they go to live somewhere. Maybe they start fresh and go where they have never been, or they may go to the community that was home before they were imprisoned. For a number of people, that is fine as long as it is "not in my backyard." Not in my backyard, or NIMBY for short, is a saying many people use to mean they do not want a certain type of person, or group of people near them. Those types might include people who live in a halfway house or rehabilitation center.

When people learn the identity of child molesters, the situation can turn dangerous. This occurred even before Megan's Law highlighted the whereabouts of sex offenders. In 1977, for example, three women in Ohio broke into the home of a convicted child molester and tied him up. That was the beginning of the torture. They then attacked him sexually, shaved his head and other body hair, and used markers to write, "I am a child molester" on areas of his body.

He was then taken from the home and left about seventy miles away.[9]

In another case, the father of a molested boy, and a friend of his, kidnapped the suspected attacker, a Louisiana teenager. They beat him with a tennis racket and sexually brutalized him.[10]

Some sex offenders whose identities were revealed under Megan's Law have been threatened, physically abused, and forced from their homes and employment by neighbors and others. In one instance, the residence to which a Washington State child rapist planned to move was burned down after authorities notified the community about him.[11]

Worse, sometimes people unknowingly go after the wrong person. For example, a New Jersey resident broke into the home of a neighbor identified by police as a sex offender. The resident attacked a man sleeping on a couch, but that man turned out not to be the offender.

After serving eleven years for a girl's murder, a Texas man could not find a place to live. He was pushed from six towns and turned away from more than a couple of hundred halfway houses.[12]

Sometimes, sex offenders take drastic measures rather than live with the backlash from the community. In Maine, for example, convicted sex offender Thomas Varnum, age thirty-one, shot himself to death after his neighbors were told of his past. He left a tape-recorded suicide note at his landlord's door that said he could not live in a world in which there was no forgiveness.[13] Varnum served nearly four years in prison for molesting two nine-year-old boys. He was released in June 1996.

Sally Sutton of the Maine Civil Liberties Union said people need to think about the consequences of notification laws.

"When we talk about public safety, we're talking about the safety of these offenders as well," she said.[14]

Sex Offenders Are an International Problem

The problem of how to cope with sex offenders is not unique to the United States. In Canada, a man named Billy Elliott was imprisoned for raping a baby. Upon release, Elliott was ostracized when he moved to a quiet family-oriented town called Eastons Corners. Signs went up giving the sex offender's address and warning people to protect themselves against him.[15]

Residents in the town of Strathmore, east of Calgary, spray-painted a motel where they thought a sex offender rented a room. The offender ended up moving.[16] However, running a child molester out of town does not necessarily work. The offender ends up going to another community, where other children could face danger. Sex offenders are also much more likely to go "underground" when confronted with the negative treatment.

Do not "sit back and say, 'Boy, we ran him out of town, now our kids are safe,'" said Detective Sergeant Brian Haggith of the Ontario Provincial Police. "Your kids are not safe."[17]

Those offenders will move elsewhere where they

may commit more crimes, especially if they do not get any community support or treatment, some experts believe.

Across Canada, volunteers called Circles of Support keep an eye on high-risk offenders, mostly by contacting them daily, to help them fit into the communities where they live.

Megan's Law: A False Sense of Security?

Another strong criticism of Megan's Law is that it can give people a false sense of security.

"If we make it hard to live openly, they'll find a way to live secretly," said Vincent Guarnaccia, a psychology professor at Hofstra University in Hempstead, New York.[18]

A study by Dr. Fred Berlin, a professor at the Johns Hopkins School of Medicine's Department of Psychiatry and Behavioral Sciences in Baltimore, Maryland revealed that out of more than six hundred sex offenders in treatment, 92 percent had no sex-abuse convictions over the five years following their release.

"The sex offenders I've worked with who make it do so because they're able to make a fresh start," said Dr. Berlin, also founder of the Johns Hopkins Sexual Disorders Clinic.[19]

Many people argue that laws protecting children against sex offenders are not adequate. There needs to be treatment for these offenders. A sex offender from Long Island, New York, quoted by *The New*

York Times in May 1999, compared a sex offense to "a runny nose."

"You don't just treat that; you treat the cold," said the man, who gave his name as Fred. Fred, who was in treatment at the time of the interview, said he deserved to be punished for his crime, but also recognized for how far he has come.[20]

Sex Offenders Speak Out About Megan's Law

In 1994, before Megan's Law was enacted in New Jersey, the state legislature listened to people, including victims, talk about their feelings on community notification. Two former sex offenders gave their opinions in writing. One of them, who called himself "Tom," said he supported registering former sexual offenders with police, but he was against telling the public.

Tom wrote:

> My crime was rape. They may decide that someone ever in jail for rape deserves to have the community notified, I don't think it's fair. I worked hard to rehabilitate myself, and it took a long time. I served a little more than 13 years. I don't think a guy who maxes out [completes his sentence, without benefit of parole] and makes no attempt to rehabilitate himself is in the same category.[21]

He and another former offender who wrote in said they were inmates with Jesse Timmendequas at the Adult Diagnostic and Treatment Center in Avenel.

The other ex-offender, who gave himself the alias Jason, said: "The only thing that really makes the community safe is effective treatment. The solution is—You don't release someone who didn't do treatment." He said he believed the likelihood of repeat crimes for those helped through therapy was very low.[22]

Jason said he met a few sex offenders while in the Avenel prison who he believed should not be released. Those prisoners did not accept responsibility for their actions and they were a probable risk if let out of prison.

"Jesse Timmendequas was one of these offenders," he said.[23]

Some Say Megan's Law Is Not Enough to Protect Children

While designed with good intentions, Megan's Law will not bring back the little girl the law is named after or protect other children, columnist Jim Breig wrote in *U.S. Catholic* magazine.

"Warning parents about

Jesse Timmendequas, ultimately sentenced to death for the murder of seven-year-old Megan Kanka, sat in a New Jersey courtroom on January 13, 1997.

a potential threat to their children is a worthwhile goal, but Megan's Law is so unconstitutional that it can't survive a serious challenge in the courts," he said.[24]

Breig said he believes the law will not rehabilitate sex offenders. He said that forcing child molesters to register after they are released from prison, and being subjected to the community notification process, means they continue to pay for their crime.

"We easily label them, to use the words of several New York politicians, as 'fiends, monsters, and predators,' but we shy away from taking the more difficult road of offering counseling and making sure they take part in it as a condition of their release from prison," Breig added.[25]

One of the many questions raised by Megan's Law critics is, Why limit the registration to just child molesters? How about burglars or drug dealers or others conducting illegal activities? What if police had to notify neighbors about the most hardened criminals?

Certainly, the knowledge of having criminals in the area may prompt residents to be extra cautious. If neighbors knew a burglar lived next door or down the street, maybe they would be less likely to leave their front door open. They might double-check window and door locks before leaving the house and while at home. Maybe they would even invest in an alarm system to protect themselves.

If a convicted drug dealer lived in the community, police could keep a better eye on his or her whereabouts. Community watch groups can also do their part to monitor street activity.

On the flip side, if burglars, drug dealers, and other offenders had to register, the paperwork piled onto law enforcement agencies could mount. Not only could it take away from handling cases, but it could also be expensive. The number of employees needed to register offenders, then notify residents, might become overwhelming.

Moreover, there is a danger that notification laws could be taken to the next level, requiring community warnings for less and less serious crimes. Where would the line be drawn before people's civil rights are put in jeopardy?

Breig said: "The people you deal with on a daily basis at work might appreciate knowing that you are quick to anger or slow to forgive or have a roving eye or a foul mouth."[26]

7

How Megan's Law Works In and Out of the Courtroom

When New Jersey Governor Christine Todd Whitman signed a nine-bill package nicknamed Megan's Law in 1994, she had a goal: "To create a system of protection for the community at large as well as to enhance our ability to deal with individuals who commit crimes of this nature."[1]

Since then, Megan's Law has been studied in detail, dissected, reviewed, challenged, revised, and praised. But is the law effective? New Jersey's action did, in fact, gain national attention which ultimately led to President Bill Clinton signing a federal version of the law. Overall, the law helped increase a community's knowledge of convicted child molesters who moved into their neighborhoods.

Taking a look at where the law came from may be a way of seeing how or if it has helped cut down on sexual crimes against children.

New Jersey's Megan's Law: Where It All Started

The historic Megan's Law bills signed into law in New Jersey addressed sex crimes against children and notification of the presence of released offenders. One of the law's major supporters came from Megan's hometown—State Senator Peter Inverso, a

Republican from Mercer County and a Hamilton Township resident. The senator helped turn the family tragedy into a way to help children every-where.

The Megan's Law bills signed by Governor

Senator Peter A. Inverso, a resident of Megan's hometown of Hamilton, New Jersey, supports putting home addresses, photos, and other information about convicted sex offenders on the Internet.

Whitman on October 31, 1994, dealt with a range of issues and concerns about how sex offenders are handled when released from prison. Some of the bills focus on the more publicized requirements, such as community notification and registration. One bill says the Department of Corrections or the Department of Human Services must provide written notification to a county prosecutor prior to the release of an adult or juvenile convicted of certain offenses, including murder and sex crimes. Another

After signing Megan's Law, President Bill Clinton met with the Kanka family of Hamilton Township, New Jersey, in the White House Oval Office on May 17, 1996. From left: Megan's sister, Jessica, 13; her parents, Richard and Maureen; and her brother, Jeremy, 10.

bill says sex offenders need to register with a designated registration agency or the chief law enforcement officer of the community where the person lives.

The remaining bills cover a variety of topics, including community supervision for life for convicted sex offenders and an extended prison term for a sex offender if the crime involved violence and if the victim was sixteen years old or younger. Also, people convicted of sexual offenses must provide samples of blood for DNA profiling and for use in connection with criminal investigations.[2]

Law Creates Awareness

Detective Darwin "Bill" Kieffer III said Megan's Law helps law enforcement officers with their cases. First, blood samples from convicted sex offenders for DNA profiling may be able to help police pinpoint a suspect, or rule someone out, based on his or her genetic code. Second, Detective Kieffer said, notification "makes us aware of who's in town."[3]

In New Jersey, the impact of Megan's Law can be seen by the growing number of sex offenders registered across the state. This helps law enforcement officers learn of convicted offenders in their communities. Here is a look at the increase in registration over the years:

- January 9, 1997, 3,532 registered offenders
- January 15, 1998, 4,760 registered offenders
- February 26, 1999, 5,834 registered offenders
- February 29, 2000, 6,638 registered offenders[4]

Police and other law enforcement agencies can keep track of sex offenders through registration. What does registration actually mean? In New Jersey, the offender is told of his Megan's Law status before being released from prison. The prisoner is also told that he needs to register with the police department in the town where he plans to live.

The prosecutor in the county where the offender expects to live gets a notice of the prisoner's release date, photographs, fingerprints, prison records, and other information. Data, including photographs and fingerprints, are then sent to the state police.

When the offender checks in with the local police department after his release, he fills out several forms for authorities and has his fingerprints and picture taken. Before the offender leaves, police will know where he lives and works, his next of kin, and his vehicle registration.

Authorities later determine whether to classify the offender as a Tier I (lowest risk), Tier II (moderate risk) or Tier III (highest risk) offender. This classification determines what type of community notification is needed for that offender. Offenders can challenge the category in which they are placed in the courts. If an offender decides not to register, then he may face up to eighteen months in jail.

Washington State Study Examines Notification

In Washington State, researchers have discovered that repeat sex offenders are being captured sooner, on average at one year out of prison compared with five years before notification laws were passed. This may be related to the police putting notices in screen doors and holding news conferences to announce an offender coming to a community.[5]

A 1997 report from the Washington State Institute for Public Policy examined the state and federal legislation dealing with Megan's Law. At that time, forty-seven states had their own versions of Megan's Law on the books, with Nebraska, Kentucky, and New Mexico being the only exceptions. Since then, those three states have adopted the law.

While New Mexico enacted a version of Megan's Law last, the state already had the 1995 Sex Offender Registration Act on the books. That law required convicted sex offenders to register their address with sheriff's offices. When Megan's Law was signed in 1999, the registration of certain offenders was made public.

After Megan's Law became official in New Mexico, Megan's mother, Maureen Kanka, sent a letter to lawmakers voicing her support for even tougher sex offender legislation sponsored by Republicans. For example, Republicans wanted law enforcement officials to let child-care centers and schools know when a sex offender moves within a mile of them. Also, the proposal would give the Department of Public Safety permission to set up a Web site featuring information about sex offenders.

However, State Representative Mimi Stewart (Democrat–Albuquerque) said: "We certainly don't want some of these offenders' names and addresses broadcast on the Internet where anyone can access it when their crime might have been something that was fairly minor."[6]

The bills strengthening the law passed in the New Mexico State Senate in February 2000.

New Mexico Strengthens Its Megan's Law

The New Mexico government responded to Kanka's request. Governor Gary Johnson signed an updated Megan's Law. In general terms, the law's enhanced version says that sheriffs must notify schools and day care centers of any sex offender living within a one-mile radius, lets the Department of Public Safety set up a Web site listing the names of sex offenders, and strengthens the communication between the Department of Public Safety and the local sheriffs' departments for notification. Also, the law expands the list of crimes requiring registration to include kidnapping and false imprisonment when the victim is under eighteen years old.[7]

One of the concerns of New Mexico's original version of Megan's Law was that the public notification process applied to crimes committed after the law took effect on July 1, 1999. The revised law applies to crimes committed back to July 1, 1995.

The way a community is notified of a sex offender can vary from state to state. For instance, in some states people are told about the release of all sex offenders from prison. In other states, notification is permitted when officials believe it is necessary to protect the public from a specific offender.

Several states notify the public based on the offender's level of risk to commit the crime again, reserving notification for those determined to be high-risk. Some states use advisory committees to help determine the risk of an offender; others require the sentencing court to assess the danger level. At least ten states use what are called "risk assessment instruments" to decide an offender's likelihood to reoffend. Point values are given to that offender's past criminal acts, the seriousness of the offenses, and behavior afterwards, among other factors. Offenders scoring a certain level are subject to community notification.

Some states, including California, Florida, New York, and Wisconsin even kept telephone numbers available so the public could find out about registered sex offenders living in their neighborhoods, according to the Washington state report.[8]

State Laws Authorizing Notification

What does each state do to enforce Megan's Law? How do police notify the community? The Washington State report on Megan's Law reviewed how states dealt with notification of convicted sex offenders. Many of the states share similar ways of handling the distribution of information, including using fliers, the media, and the World Wide Web to alert the public to sex offenders living in a community.

For example, in California, where Megan's Law was enacted in 1996, information about high-risk offenders may be released through news organizations. Serious sex offender information may be provided to public and private schools, day care centers, people likely to encounter the offender, and other agencies which serve people likely to be victimized by the offender. For someone to be a high-risk offender, he or she has to meet certain criteria including being convicted of three or more violent sex offenses or having a conviction of two violent sex offenses and one or more violent nonsexual offenses.

In an effort to protect sex offenders, warnings are given through a "900" phone line and CD–ROM that it is illegal to use the information to commit a crime against people listed or to harass or illegally discriminate against them.

In Florida, where Megan's Law was enacted in 1995, then revised a year later, sex offender information is also available through an "800" telephone line and through the World Wide Web. Notices include the offender's name, description (including a photograph), offense and circumstances surrounding the conviction, and whether the victim was a minor or adult at the time of the offense. The courts in Florida consider a lot of information when deciding whether an offender is at risk. This includes the relationship between the predator and the victim, response to treatment, whether violence or weapons or the threat of violence were used, and if there are any prior sexual or violent offenses.[9]

Upholding Megan's Law

None of the state laws are identical, although many have a lot of similarities. Legal fights challenging Megan's Law have generally been unsuccessful. However, in several states, courts have ruled that applying the law to people who committed a sexual crime before Megan's Law took effect was unconstitutional. More recently, higher courts such as the U.S. Court of Appeals have decided that the law can be applied retroactively.[10] This can be seen in New Mexico, where the law was strengthened in February 2000 to include sex offenders who committed crimes back to July 1, 1995.

Other laws also help law enforcement officers stay aware of sex offenders as they move within and outside of a state. For example, the Pam Lychner Sexual Offender Tracking and Identification Act of 1996 called for the development of a central location where information about sex offenders would be kept. This was meant to help the FBI track offenders when they move. The law says that the FBI had to establish the national database of sex offenders within three years; the database was set up and began operating on schedule in the summer of 1999.

The management of the database contains five basic steps:

1. States send information about sex offenders to the FBI.

2. The FBI adds this information to the existing criminal history record system.

3. Law enforcement officials perform a routine criminal history check on an individual and receive a record that includes sex offender information submitted by the state.

4. Law enforcement follows the lead from the criminal history record and contacts the state registry. That means the records will help point law

Here is an overall view of what the National Crime Information Center at the Federal Bureau of Investigation headquarters in Washington, D.C., looked like in 1967. At that time, the computers did not hold missing persons information; that data was added on October 1, 1975.

enforcement officials to the appropriate state registry or registries if they need more information.

5. Law enforcement uses the National Law Enforcement Telecommunications System (NLETS) to share sex offender registry information. States can electronically search and get data from the registry, as well as get information by telephone, e-mail, or regular mail.[11]

President Clinton said a national database sends a simple message to people who prey on children: "The law will follow you wherever you go."[12] In an August 1996 radio address, the president talked about the importance of stopping sexual predators, keeping track of them, and reducing crimes against children:

> Above all, we must move forward to the day when we are no longer numb to acts of violence against children, when their appearance on the evening news is both shocking and very rare. Our approach is working. We're putting cops on the beat; taking guns, drugs, and criminals off the streets. More and more, our children can learn and play and dream without risk of harm. That is an America that is moving in the right direction.[13]

8

Teaching Children to Watch Out for Themselves

When it comes to protecting children against child molesters, sometimes advice comes from an unusual source. For example, a child molester wrote to Ann Landers offering his suggestions on how children can be safeguarded from pedophiles.

Here is his letter, as published in June 1999:

> Dear Ann Landers: I am your average, everyday child molester. Please understand that I'm not talking about a guy who hides behind bushes or hangs around schoolyards and playgrounds. I could be anyone—your neighbor,

your friend, your brother, your father, even your grandfather. I am the guy who becomes your friend so I can get close to your child.

Ann, the best warning I can give your readers is this: If an adult is spending a lot of time with your child, there is a reason, and it's probably a bad one. Why else would an adult want to take your child to the movies, to the mall, to video arcades, to the swimming pool, to car races, to amusement parks or on overnight camping trips? Be alert to any adult who is giving your child a lot of special attention and is willing to take him or her anywhere. That adult may seem kind and helpful, but believe me, there could be a motive behind the kindness.

If this is happening to your children, you need to start asking questions. And be aware that children could lie to you about what's going on because they are afraid the molester will harm them or they will get into trouble with you, their parents. When I was molested as a child, I lied to my father when he asked about it because I was afraid he would punish me. Had I told him, the molestation surely would have stopped, and I would have received help. Instead, the molesting went on for years. It destroyed my life and the lives of others because I became a molester and did the same things that were done to me.

I prey mostly on the children of single mothers, who welcome someone who will take their child off their hands for a while, and they like the father figure I provide. The children welcome me because I act like a big kid myself and take them places they enjoy. If your child is lonesome, he is the perfect target for a pedophile.

Whoever is reading this, please think about what is going on in your family. If you are a grandparent, consider your son or daughter's household. If everyone would just take the time to talk to their children, thousands of kids could be spared the trauma, heartache, and pain that a pedophile can create. A molester can also turn the child into a pedophile, too. A molested kid has a 1–in–4 chance of becoming a molester. I know this is true because it happened to me.

Carefully ask your child questions that will get truthful answers. Don't put any blame on the child. Show children you care about them. And remember this red flag: If an adult is going out of his way to spend time with your child, find out why. Something may be wrong.

—No Name, No City

Dear No Name: Here is your letter, which is sure to generate some negative responses from adult males who fit your description but will deny there is anything unwholesome about their relationship with the children they befriend.[1]

Basic Safety Rules for Children

Diligence, knowledge, and common sense can all help in the effort to protect children from harm.

Peter Banks shuddered when he recalled the day his daughter, two years old at the time, disappeared in a Virginia drugstore.

"I had been a policeman back then; you think of the worst things," he said in March 2000.[2]

Thankfully, the worst did not happen at that strip mall nineteen years before. A customer found his little girl next door at a Kmart register with a candy bar.

While many missing children, like Banks's daughter Meredith, are found safe and sound, some can fall prey to sex offenders and others who may want to hurt children. Banks knows all too well what can happen to children who get lost in busy places such as malls, amusement parks, and fairs while on vacation, and even in their own neighborhoods. As director of training and outreach for The National Center for Missing and Exploited Children (NCMEC), he said parents need to teach their children what to do if they lose their way.

According to the NCMEC, as soon as children can articulate a sentence, they can begin to learn how to protect themselves against abduction and exploitation. Here are some tips young people should try to learn:

- If a child is in a public place and gets separated from his or her parents, that child should not wander around looking for them. The child should go to a checkout counter, the security office, or the lost and found and tell the person in charge that help is needed to find mom and dad.
- Children should not get into a car or go anywhere with any person unless their parents have told them that it is all right.

- Children need to stay away from a person who follows them on foot or in a car. The child should not go near the car to talk to the people inside.

- Grown-ups and other older people who need help should be asking other adults, not children.

- A child should not be asked for directions or for help finding a "lost puppy." No one should be telling a child that a parent is in trouble and that he or she will take the child to the parent.

- If someone tries to take a child somewhere, that child should quickly get away from him (or her) and yell or scream: "This man (or woman) is trying to take me away," or "This person is not my father (or mother)."

- Children should try to use the "buddy system" (sticking with another child) and never go places alone.

- Children should always ask a parent's permission to leave the yard or play area or to go into someone's home.

- Children should never hitchhike or try to get a ride home with anyone unless their parents have told them it is okay to ride with that person.

- No one should ask a child to keep a special secret. If he or she does, that child should tell his or her parents or teacher.

- If someone wants to take a picture of a child, tell him or her NO. The child should then inform his or her parents or a teacher.

- No one should touch a child in the parts of the body covered by the bathing suit, nor should a youngster touch anyone else in those areas. The body is special and private.

- Children can be assertive and they have the right to say NO to someone who tries to take them somewhere, touch them, or make them feel uncomfortable in any way.[3]

Adults Can Help Children Protect Themselves

Here is what the NCMEC says adults can do to help prevent child abduction and exploitation:

- Parents should know where their children are at all times and be familiar with their friends and daily activities.

- Adults need to be sensitive to changes in their children's behavior; those changes are a signal that parents should sit down and talk to the children about what caused the changes.

- Parents should be alert to a teenager or adult who is paying an unusual amount of attention to their children or giving them inappropriate or expensive gifts.

- Children need to be taught to trust their own feelings and be assured that they have the right to say NO to what they sense is wrong.

- Parents need to listen carefully to their children's fears and be supportive in all discussions with them.

- Children need to learn that no one should approach them or touch them in a way that makes them feel uncomfortable. If someone does, they should tell the parents immediately.

- Adults need to be careful about baby-sitters and any other individuals who have custody of their children.[4]

Foundations Help Parents Fight Abduction

People cope with the death of a child in many ways. The Kanka family, similar to others of murdered or missing children, formed a foundation in their child's memory, pushed for laws against sexual offenders, and spoke out on preventing violence against children. For example, Colleen Nick, whose six-year-old daughter, Morgan, disappeared at an Alma, Arkansas, ball field on June 9, 1995, formed the Morgan Nick Foundation. Morgan was catching fireflies in a parking lot near the field when she vanished. The foundation has done many things, such as supporting Megan's Law.[5]

Shortly after Megan's death, Maureen and Richard formed the Megan Nicole Kanka Foundation. The foundation offers scholarships and educational classes through school-parent organizations and police crime prevention units.[6]

Maureen Kanka continues to speak to the public not only about Megan's Law, but also about how people can protect their own children. In March 2000, the foundation cosponsored a program with the Clara Maass Medical Center in New Jersey called "Who Is Watching Our Children?"

Another foundation, called the Adam Walsh Children's Fund, is the educational and fund-raising division of The National Center for Missing and Exploited Children. The Children's Fund was named for six-year-old Adam Walsh, who was abducted and murdered in Florida.

Two foundations exist for Polly Klaas. The Polly Klaas Foundation was formed in 1993 to help search for twelve-year-old Polly, who was kidnapped from her California home and brutally murdered. After her body was found, the organization came up with a new mission that includes helping find missing children, educating the public to prevent crimes against youngsters, and supporting laws that protect children. The KlaasKids Foundation was founded in 1994 by Polly's father, Marc Klaas, to encourage partnerships between neighborhoods, law enforcement agencies, and organizations to help create safe communities. The foundation also supports laws that protect children from abuse, neglect, and abduction.

The Jacob Wetterling Foundation was established in February 1990, four months after eleven-year-old Jacob was abducted near his home in St. Joseph, Minnesota. Jacob's parents, Jerry and Patty Wetterling, started the nonprofit foundation to bring national attention to missing children and their families. Jacob is still missing.

Rosemarie D'Alessandro, whose daughter Joan was raped and murdered at the hands of a neighbor in Hillsdale, New Jersey, in 1973, formed the Joan Angela D'Alessandro Memorial Foundation in the summer of 1998. The organization was set up to help pay for past and future expenses in the fight to oppose Joan's killer's parole and support Joan's Law. That law says that anyone who molests and murders a child under fourteen years old cannot get parole.

In the year 2000, D'Alessandro began pushing for another law, a proposed Justice For Victims Law. If the legislature approves the bill, families of murder victims could have an easier time suing for money inherited by convicted murderers.[7] Joan's killer, Joseph McGowan, received an inheritance after his parents died in the 1990s, and he used the money to pay for lawyers. The D'Alessandros, on the other hand, spent their own money to fight his appeals.[8]

Rosemarie D'Alessandro said she wants the law to apply retroactively to her family. She believes victims should have access to this money.[9]

"This bill will give the victims some justice," she said. "It will give them the chance to get the moneys from the criminals and they can use it in constructive ways while the criminals will use it for their appeals, which is what happened to us."[10]

In June 2000, the bill jumped over its first hurdle—the state Assembly's Judiciary Committee passed it unanimously. The bill is expected to move to the Senate for a vote. If the Senate approves it, the bill goes to the governor, who then decides whether to sign it into law.

Remembering Megan

Besides foundations, there are other ways families remember their lost children. For Megan Kanka, a park also helps preserve her memory.

Trees, a bench, a fountain, and a pond with fish sit on the property once occupied by a house where convicted child molester Jesse Timmendequas lived.

A wooden birdhouse with the name "Megan" carved in it and a small attached photograph of the little girl serves as a reminder of the life that was cut too short in the summer of 1994. Next to the pond under a tree rests an angel statue.

The Rotary Club of Hamilton–Washington Townships bought the two-story home, where Timmendequas and his roommates had lived, for $100,000. The Rotary raised most of the money to buy the house through donations. The home was torn down in December 1994, about five months after

The Rotary Club of Hamilton–Washington Townships raised thousands of dollars in donations to buy the home where Megan was murdered and convert the property into a park called Megan's Place.

Megan was murdered there, and the land was later converted into a park. The park is called "Megan's Place."[11] The Rotary later raised additional donations from all over the United States to pay back a loan and create a fund to maintain the park.

The day of the demolition, Megan's then nine-year-old brother Jeremy said: "The park is going to feel much better than the house. When I looked at the house, it reminded me of Megan getting killed."[12]

Megan's mother, Maureen Kanka, said: "I know she's going to smile down on everything."[13]

Protecting Children: An Ongoing Education

Megan's story shows that a child molester can be right across the street. Or an attacker can come right into the home. In Polly's case, the man who murdered her was a complete stranger who snuck into her bedroom and took her

The murder of Megan Kanka brought an outpouring of support from across the United States and elsewhere. Here, a plaque from the Rotary Club of Campinas Alvorada, Brazil, presented in June 1998, commemorated a corner of the park named after the seven-year-old girl.

away during what should have been a fun, safe evening—a slumber party among friends.

Child molesters are also invading the Internet. With millions of children online talking in chat rooms, predators have access to youngsters at the click of a mouse. Sometimes children may think they are talking with another child when they are, in fact, chatting with an adult who may be set out to harm them.

In April 2000, Representative Bob Franks of New Jersey's Seventh Congressional District called for tougher sentences for cyber-molesters. He proposed a mandatory prison term for anyone who uses the Internet to lure children into sex.

"Tragically, in increasing numbers, children are being victimized by cyber-molesters. The FBI reports a 550 percent increase in these cases over the last two years," the congressman said. "Imposing a mandatory prison term for high-tech child molesters

Representative Bob Franks of New Jersey's Seventh Congressional District called for stricter sentences for sexual predators who "meet" children on the Internet.

is the very least we can do to protect our children from the growing and significant threat to their safety."[14]

The percentage seems alarming. However, the number is high because the Internet is still relatively new, and the FBI in recent years began dedicating more resources to catching online molesters. In response to online child sexual exploitation, the FBI in 1995 created Innocent Images, a nationwide program. Chat rooms can give molesters an anonymity that may help them recruit youngsters into sexual relationships. The FBI has investigated more than seventy cases in which offenders have traveled across state lines to meet a child.[15]

Learning from Megan's Law

A stroll down Barbara Lee Drive, where Megan's life was cut short in 1994, serves as a reminder that crimes against children can occur virtually anywhere—even in places where people could be heard to say, "That could never happen here."

The strength of Megan's close-knit community, and especially of her parents, helped create national awareness of problems relating to sex offenders. Megan's Law, or the right of neighbors to know when a convicted child molester moves onto their block, continues to make news. The law prompts strong opinions, with some people saying that children need to be protected at all costs. Others argue that the law not only violates the offender's right to privacy, but also makes that person continue paying for a crime after serving the time.

A hopscotch court rested prominently at Megan's Place, a park named after Hamilton Township, New Jersey, murder victim, Megan Kanka. Hopscotch was said to be a favorite game.

Children need to feel safe in their homes, in their schools, and around their neighborhoods. However, they also need to understand, as best as possible, how to react and be aware of danger. Maybe that asks them to become adults too soon, to recognize at an early age that someone may not be acting out of kindness or in their best interests. Armed with knowledge, children may have a better chance of steering clear of the dangers of sex offenders so that they can do what victims Megan, Polly, and Adam will never get to do—grow up.

Appendix

Here is a basic overview of the Megan's Law bills signed by New Jersey Governor Christine Todd Whitman on October 31, 1994:

- Assembly No. 165 requires the Department of Corrections or the Department of Human Services to provide written notification to a county prosecutor prior to the release of an adult or juvenile convicted or judged delinquent of certain offenses. These include murder and sexual crimes. The prosecutor then is required to notify the Office of Victim–Witness Advocacy.

- Assembly No. 84 requires the registration of sex offenders with a designated registration agency or the chief law enforcement officer of the community where the person lives.

- Senate No. 14 and Assembly No. 85 provide for community notification when a sex offender is released from an institution and moves into a town. The community notification is to be given in accordance with guidelines developed by the attorney general.

- Senate No. 320 sets up community supervision for life for convicted sex offenders. Community supervision will begin upon the offender's release and the monitoring system is similar to that used for parolees.

- Senate Nos. 11, 902, and Assembly No. 82 provide for an extended prison term for a sexual offender if the crime involved violence and if the victim was sixteen years old or less.

- Senate No. 15 says that no inmate at the Adult Diagnostic and Treatment Center at Avenel will be eligible for good behavior credit unless that person cooperates with the treatment program offered there.

- Assembly No. 1592 requires people convicted of sexual offenses to provide samples of blood for DNA profiling and use in connection with criminal investigations.

- Assembly No. 81 establishes a victim's age of less than fourteen years old as an aggravating factor in death penalty cases.

- Assembly No. 86 provides for the involuntary commitment of sex offenders whose conduct has been characterized by a pattern of repetitive, compulsive behavior.

Afterword

What happened years ago to murdered children such as Megan Kanka and Joan D'Alessandro continues to affect parents, neighborhoods, and the legal system today.

For example, in the November 7, 2000, election, New Jersey residents headed to the polls not only to vote for a United States president and local officials, but to consider a constitutional change relating to sex offenders. Voters overwhelmingly supported an amendment that would give the state legislature permission to authorize the disclosure of the identity, general and specific whereabouts, physical characteristics, and criminal history of those who have committed a sex offense.

This vote helps open the door for a New Jersey sex offender registry on the World Wide Web. That means that anyone using the Internet can find out the names and addresses, as well as other information, about sex offenders. With that information, angry people could conceivably attack offenders, or offenders might lose their jobs. But those in favor of the law say the public's right to know overrides the right to privacy of sex offenders.

Another new proposal, known as the Justice for Victims Law, was approved in New Jersey in the year 2000. A bill that lets murder victims' families sue for wrongful death suits at any time was signed into law by Acting Governor Donald T. DiFrancesco. Under the previous law, an action for wrongful death had to be brought within two years of the victim's death.

"This new law addresses the inherent difficulty for families to consider future litigation when they are dealing with the loss of a loved one, focusing on criminal investigations or ongoing trials," DiFrancesco said.

Rosemarie D'Alessandro, mother of Joan D'Alessandro, who was murdered in 1973 by a neighbor, discovered years after her daughter's death that the two-year statute prevented her from suing convicted killer Joseph McGowan. McGowan had reportedly received a large inheritance that he was using for his appeals. DiFrancesco signed the bill on November 17, 2000, in Hillsdale, D'Alessandro's hometown.

"There is no statute of limitation on pain and grief for the family of a murder or manslaughter victim. And for many, there is no resolution even after a trial has ended," DiFrancesco said. "It can take time for families to come to terms with how and when they want to pursue appropriate litigation, and this new law gives them the time they need."

Meanwhile, as of January 2001, McGowan was serving a life sentence at the New Jersey State Prison in Trenton. Megan's killer, Jesse Timmendequas, was on death row at the same prison awaiting execution.

Chapter Notes

Chapter 1. A Child's Murder Shocks the Nation and Sparks Change

1. Dale Russakoff and Blaine Harden, "Megan's killer sentenced to death: Jury finds repeat sex offender's childhood suffering did not lessen responsibility," *The Washington Post*, June 21, 1997, p. A3.

2. Thomas Zambito, "Mom recalls Megan's last day: First witness in Timmendequas' trial," *The* (Bergen) *Record*, May 6, 1997, p. A1.

3. Tom Hester, "Execution debate set for June 9: Jurors glare at Megan's killer before eight convictions are read," *The* (Newark) *Star-Ledger*, May 31, 1997, p. 1 (State section).

4. James Barron, "Vigil for slain girl, 7, Backs a law on offenders," *New York Times* abstracts, August 3, 1994, p. 4.

5. Timothy D. May, "Megan's Law: How it works in real life—Police, prosecutors have difficult task," *The* (Bergen) *Record*, March 14, 1999, p. A1.

6. Rick Hampson, "What's gone wrong with Megan's Law? Notification: Reason for law is its biggest problem," *USA Today*, May 14, 1997, p. 1A.

7. Scott Matson with Roxanne Lieb, "Megan's Law: A Review of State and Federal Legislation," Washington State Institute for Public Policy, October 1997, pp. 27–28.

8. Ivette Mendez, "Megan's tragedy touched public's heart, brought change to protect kids," *The* (Newark) *Star-Ledger*, January 1, 1995, <www.nj.com/archive>.

9. Uniform Crime Reporting Program, Federal Bureau of Investigation, *Number of Murder Victims, Ages newborn to 12 years of age, 1989–1998*, Washington, D.C., n.d., courtesy of the Federal Bureau of Investigation.

10. Mendez.

11. Hampson, p. 1A.

12. John Walsh, with Susan Schindehette, *Tears of Rage* (New York: Pocket Books, 1997), inside front flap.

13. National Center for Missing and Exploited Children, *1998 Missing Children Statistics,* fact sheet, Alexandria, Va., n.d., courtesy of The National Center for Missing and Exploited Children.

14. James R. Kincaid, *Erotic Innocence* (Durham and London: Duke University Press, 1998), p. 181.

15. Martin L. Forst and Martha-Elin Blomquist, *Missing Children* (New York: Lexington Books, 1991), p. 85.

Chapter 2. The Birth of Megan's Law

1. Thomas Zambito, "Mom recalls Megan's last day: First witness in Timmendequas trial," *The* (Bergen) *Record*, May 6, 1997, p. A1.

2. Ibid.

3. Personal interview with Detective Darwin W. "Bill" Kieffer III, Hamilton Township Police Department, November 4, 1999.

4. Ibid.

5. Ibid.

6. Ibid.

7. Zambito, p. A1.

8. Personal interview with Detective Kieffer.

9. Ibid.

10. Ibid.

11. Ibid.

12. Ibid.

13. Ibid.

14. Ibid.

15. Ibid.

16. Ibid.

17. Ibid.

18. Ibid.

19. Ibid.

20. Ibid.

21. Ibid.

22. Ibid.

23. Zambito, p. A1.

24. William Glaberson, "Prosecution rests in Megan trial: Suspect coolly described rape, murder of girl, 7, officer testifies," *Houston Chronicle,* May 23, 1997, p. 7.

25. Ibid.

26. William Glaberson, "Defense calls no witness: 3-week trial in death of child concludes," *Houston Chronicle,* May 24, 1997, p. 14.

27. Tom Hester, "Execution debate set for June 9: Jurors glare at Megan's killer before eight convictions are read," *The* (Newark) *Star-Ledger,* May 31, 1997, p. 1.

28. Ibid.

29. Ibid.

30. Rick Hampson, "What's gone wrong with Megan's Law? Notification: Reason for law is its biggest problem," *USA Today,* May 14, 1997, p. 01A.

31. "Remarks by The President in Bill Signing Ceremony for Megan's Law," press release, Washington, D.C., May 17, 1996.

Chapter 3. History of Laws Protecting Children Against Child Molesters

1. Scott Matson with Roxanne Lieb, "Megan's Law: A Review of State and Federal Legislation," Washington State Institute for Public Policy, October 1997, p. 4.

2. Personal interview with Roxanne Lieb, director, Washington State Institute for Public Policy, Olympia, Washington, March 21, 2000.

3. Scott Matson, "Sex Offender Registration: Policy Overview and Comprehensive Practices," Madeline M. Carter, ed., Center for Sex Offender Management, October 1999, p. 2.

4. Matson, p. 13.

5. National Center for Missing and Exploited Children and the Office of Juvenile Justice and Delinquency Prevention, Office of Justice Programs, U.S. Department of Justice, *Children at Risk,* Alexandria, Va., n.d., courtesy of The National Center for Missing and Exploited Children.

6. National Center for Missing and Exploited Children and Adam Walsh Children's Fund, *1996–1997 Annual Report, For the Children*, Alexandria, Va., n.d., courtesy of The National Center for Missing and Exploited Children, p. 4.

7. Ibid., p. 2.

8. Michael Rubinkam, "Parents of slain student push for tougher interstate parole statutes," *The Harrisburg Patriot*, October 7, 1998, p. B4.

9. U.S. Representative Matt Salmon, "Advocating 'Aimee's Law'," *The Washington Post*, May 15, 1999, Letters to the Editor, p. A22.

10. Rubinkam, p. B4.

11. Ibid.

12. Bruce Alpert, "'Aimee's Law' wins approval in Senate: It would punish states for releasing inmates who commit crimes elsewhere," *The New Orleans Times-Picayune*, May 20, 1999, p. A13.

13. Personal interview with Rosemarie D'Alessandro, December 15, 1999.

14. Jerry Jastrab, "Hillsdale murderer up for parole," *Community Life*, August 11, 1993, pp. 1, 8, 36.

15. Ibid.

16. Personal interview with Michael J. D'Alessandro, December 15, 1999.

17. Personal interview with Rosemarie D'Alessandro.

Chapter 4. Portrait of a Child Molester

1. Kenneth V. Lanning, "Child Molesters: A Behavioral Analysis For Law Enforcement Officers Investigating Cases of Child Sexual Exploitation," National Center for Missing and Exploited Children (in cooperation with the Federal Bureau of Investigation), December 1992, pp. 2–3.

2. ChildAbuse.com, "Why Child Abuse Occurs & Criminal Background of the Perpetrator," 1999, <http://www.childabuse.com/perp.htm> (December 24, 1999).

3. Mary Jane Fine, "From prey to predator?—Experts split on effect of sexual abuse," *The* (Bergen) *Record*, March 27, 1998, p. A1.

4. Lanning, p. 16.

5. Ann Wolbert Burgess, R.N., D.N.Sc., and Christine A. Grant, R.N., Ph.D, "Children Traumatized in Sex Rings," a report from The National Center for Missing and Exploited Children, March 1988, p. 4.

6. Lanning, p. 8.

7. Thomas Zolper, "Megan's killer likened to time bomb: Upbringing led him to sex crime, defense says," *The* (Bergen) *Record*, June 13, 1997, p. A3.

8. Jonathan Jaffe, Jim O'Neill, and Jeff May, "Timmendequas brother is held in sex assaults: He allegedly attacked 2 girls at friend's E. Brunswick home," *The* (Newark) *Star-Ledger*, March 26, 1998, p. 1.

9. Zolper, p. A3.

10. Tom Hester, "2 portraits emerge of Megan killer: Penalty phase of trial opens showing abused and abuser," *The* (Newark) *Star-Ledger*, June 10, 1997, p. 1.

11. Donna De La Cruz, "Megan Kanka's killer pleads for his life," *The Associated Press*, June 18, 1997, <www. factiva.com>.

12. Thomas Fields-Meyer, Laird Harrison, and Gabrielle Saveri, "Odyssey of violence all his adult life, Richard Davis was a one-man crime wave. Why was he free to kill Polly Klaas?" *People*, May 13, 1996, p. 44.

13. Mary Curtius, "Polly's killer hurts family again: In final comments, Davis says girl was molested by father," *The* (Tacoma, Wash.) *News Tribune*, September 27, 1996, p. A1.

14. Steve Marshall, "Crime-victim advocates outraged: Killer's comments 'directed to break Marc Klaas' heart,'" *USA Today*, September 27, 1996, p. 3A.

15. Curtius, p. A1.

16. Marshall, p. 3A.

17. Fields-Meyer, Harrison, and Saveri, p. 44.

18. Ibid.

19. Louise Continelli, "A father fights back: UB grad John Walsh turned the unspeakable murder of his son into a lifelong crusade," *Buffalo News*, July 5, 1998, p. M16.

20. Ibid.

21. Ibid.

22. Ibid.

23. John Walsh, with Susan Schindehette, *Tears of Rage* (New York: Pocket Books, 1997), p. 57.

24. Continelli.

25. Ibid.

Chapter 5. The Case for Megan's Law: Protection

1. Michelle Ruess, "A mother's plea: Pass Megan's bill, panel OKs compromise," *The* (Bergen) *Record*, September 27, 1994, p. A1.

2. "N.J. signs laws on sex offenders," *Intelligencer* (Lancaster, Pa.) *Journal*, November 1, 1994, p. A–13.

3. Ibid.

4. "Remarks by The President in Bill Signing Ceremony for Megan's Law," press release, Washington, D.C., May 17, 1996.

5. "Officials Address Megan's Law: Hannon responds to reports of sex offender in area," *Levittown Tribune*, March 20, 1998, <http://antonnews.com/levittowntribune/1998/03/20/news> (November 16, 1999).

6. Ibid.

7. Ivette Mendez, "Senate panel approves sex-offender measures, modified notification bill," *The* (Newark) *Star-Ledger*, September 27, 1994, <www.nj.com/archive>.

8. William J. Clinton, "Development of a National Sexual Offender Registration System," Memorandum for the Attorney General, press release, Washington, D.C., June 25, 1996.

9. National Center for Missing and Exploited Children and the Office of Juvenile Justice and Delinquency Prevention, Office of Justice Programs, U.S. Department of Justice, *A Report to the Nation: Missing and Exploited Children*, Alexandria, Va., January 1997, p. 13, courtesy of The National Center for Missing and Exploited Children.

10. John P. McAlpin, "Megan's Law leads to larger DNA database," *The* (Bergen) *Record*, September 6, 2000, p. A3.

11. Ibid.

12. Michelle Ruess, "The Record Poll: Sex offender bill garners wide support but Megan's Law doesn't go far enough, many say," *The* (Bergen) *Record*, October 26, 1994, p. a01.

13. "Gov. Whitman Hails Supreme Court's Refusal to Hear Appeal of Megan's Law," press release, Office of the Governor, Trenton, N. J., February 23, 1998.

14. Ibid.

15. Jim Breig, "Labeling sex offenders won't protect children," *U.S. Catholic*, November 1996, vol. 61, no. 11, p. 13(6).

16. "A Model State Sex-Offender Policy," The National Center for Missing and Exploited Children, 1998, p. 8.

Chapter 6. The Case Against Megan's Law: Privacy Violation

1. Ralph Siegel, "Judge lifts freeze on Megan's Law," *The* (Bergen) *Record*, July 13, 2000, p. A1.

2. Christopher Mumma, "Megan's Law needs adjusting, judge says," *The* (Bergen) *Record*, January 27, 2000, p. A1.

3. Siegel, p. A1.

4. Elise Young, "U.S. judge upholds Megan's Law notice," *The* (Bergen) *Record*, September 12, 2000, p. A1.

5. Rick Hampson, "What's gone wrong with Megan's Law? Notification: Reason for law is its biggest problem," *USA Today*, May 14, 1997, p. 01A.

6. Mumma, p. A1.

7. Cynthia Blair, "Trying to sort out legalities of Megan's Law," *The New York Times*, May 16, 1999, Long Island Weekly Desk, Section 14LI, p. 2.

8. Ibid.

9. James R. Kincaid, *Erotic Innocence* (Durham and London: Duke University Press, 1998), pp. 93–94.

10. Ibid.

11. Scott Matson with Roxanne Lieb, "Megan's Law: A Review of State and Federal Legislation," Washington State Institute for Public Policy, October 1997, p. 28.

12. Hampson, p. 1A.

13. "Molester's suicide stirs debate on notification laws," *The* (Bergen) *Record*, February 16, 1998, p. A7.

14. Ibid.

15. Erin Anderssen, "The bogeyman next door. He raped a baby, did his time and came home. Now, his neighbours are trying to drive him out. But where is he supposed to go?" *The Globe and Mail*, November 9, 1999, p. A16.

16. Ibid.

17. Ibid.

18. Blair, p. 2.

19. Ibid.

20. Ibid.

21. Mary Jo Patterson, "Treated sex offenders say Megan's Law unfair: Two jailed with girl's killer assert he's one of few unable to change," *The* (Newark) *Star-Ledger,* October 2, 1994, <www.nj.com/archive>.

22. Ibid.

23. Ibid.

24. Jim Breig, "Labeling sex offenders won't protect children," *U.S. Catholic*, November 1996, vol. 61, no. 11, p. 13(6).

25. Ibid.

26. Ibid.

Chapter 7. How Megan's Law Works in and out of the Courtroom

1. Press release: Office of the Governor, Trenton, N. J., October 31, 1994.

2. Ibid., and State of New Jersey Office of Legislative Services, 1994, Sen. Nos. 11, 14, 15, 320 and 902, and Assembly Nos. 81, 82, 84, 85, 86, 165 and 1592, courtesy of the State of New Jersey Office of Legislative Services.

3. Personal interview with Detective Darwin W. "Bill" Kieffer III, Hamilton Township Police Department, November 4, 1999.

4. Office of the Attorney General, New Jersey, Public Affairs-Press Office, *Megan's Law Statistics and Megan's Law Registration*, Trenton, N.J., n.d.

5. Rick Hampson, "What's gone wrong with Megan's Law? Notification: Reason for law is its biggest problem," *USA Today*, May 14, 1997, p. 1A.

6. Barry Massey, "Megan's mom tries to help GOP toughen law in N.M.," *The Santa Fe New Mexican*, February 7, 2000, p. A–1.

7. New Mexico Department of Public Safety, *Enhanced Megan's Law*, n.d.

8. Scott Matson with Roxanne Lieb, "Megan's Law: A Review of State and Federal Legislation," Washington State Institute for Public Policy, October 1997, p. 14.

9. Ibid., pp. 36–37, 43–44.

10. Ibid., p. 29.

11. *Attorney General's Report to the President: A National Sex Offender Registry*, Washington, D.C., August 1996, courtesy of the FBI Press Office.

12. "Radio Address of the President to the Nation," press release/transcript, Washington, D.C., August 24, 1996.

13. Ibid.

Chapter 8. Teaching Children to Watch Out for Themselves

1. *The* (Bergen) *Record*, June 7, 1999, p. L10, permission granted by Ann Landers and Creators Syndicate.

2. Personal interview with Peter Banks, director of training and outreach, The National Center for Missing and Exploited Children, March 7, 2000.

3. National Center for Missing and Exploited Children, *Child Protection*, Alexandria, Va., n.d., with permission from The National Center for Missing and Exploited Children.

4. Ibid.

5. C.K. Binswanger, "When a child vanishes," *Redbook*, September 1999, p. 136.

6. "Maureen Kanka headlines 'Stranger Danger' program," *The Observer*, March 1, 2000, p. 4.

7. Deena Yellin, "The mother behind Joan's Law champions new victims measure," *The* (Bergen) *Record*, January 25, 2000, p. A4.

8. Ibid.

9. Personal interview with Rosemarie D'Alessandro, December 15, 1999.

10. Yellin, p. A4.

11. Brendan Schurr, "House where girl was slain is razed for park," *The Seattle Times*, December 25, 1994, p. A3.

12. "Neighborhood destroys house of death: Park to be built on site where 7-year-old girl was assaulted, slain," *Rocky Mountain News*, December 22, 1994, p. 56a.

13. Schurr, p. A3.

14. "Franks Calls for Tougher Sentences for Cybermolesters," press release, April 3, 2000, Office of Bob Franks, Seventh Congressional District, New Jersey.

15. *Innocent Images*, Department of Justice, Federal Bureau of Investigation, Washington, D.C., n.d., with permission from the Federal Bureau of Investigation, Press Office.

Glossary

appeal—Request that a higher court of law look at a case that has already been decided in a lower court, typically to overturn the original decision.

assault—To cause or attempt to cause bodily harm through unlawful force.

attorney general—A top law enforcement officer of the federal government or state government.

battered—Subjected to frequent violence.

bill—A proposed law to be reviewed by lawmakers.

capital punishment—Putting a criminal to death legally because he or she has murdered someone.

child molester—Someone who sexually abuses children.

death penalty—The law that allows the government to take a life.

death row—The prison cell area where those sentenced to death are held until execution.

death sentence—The decision by a judge or jury that the person convicted of a specific crime should die.

defendant—Also called the accused, a defendant is someone charged with a crime in court.

evidence—Testimony, records, documents, or other materials offered at a trial to prove or disprove something brought up in court or elsewhere.

execution—This term has many legal meanings, including the carrying out of a death sentence.

expert witness—Someone called upon in court with special knowledge or skills relating to a subject.

Federal Bureau of Investigation (FBI)—A U.S. Department of Justice agency that looks into violations of U.S. government laws, except those assigned to other organizations.

felony—A generic term used to describe certain high crimes, such as murder.

life without parole—An alternative to the death penalty, in which the offender stays in jail until he or she dies.

parole—When a person is released from prison on the condition that he or she complies with certain rules or possibly faces prison again.

pedophile—A person who has strong sexual urges and sexually arousing fantasies about a child, typically thirteen or younger.

prosecutor—A public official, a lawyer representing the government, who tries a case against someone accused of a crime. Prosecutors arguing on behalf of the state government are often called district attorneys; those arguing on behalf of the federal government are known as United States attorneys.

sentence—A punishment decided in court for someone convicted of a crime.

sex offender—A general term used to describe someone who commits a sexual crime.

unconstitutional—Not in keeping with the laws in the U.S. Constitution or any state constitution, and therefore, not considered legal.

victim—Someone who is hurt in some way by a crime.

vigilante—In general, an unauthorized group, or individuals who take it upon themselves to try to punish criminals outside the legal system.

Further Reading

Books

de Becker, Gavin. *The Gift of Fear*. New York: Dell Publishing, a division of Bantam Doubleday Dell Publishing Group, Inc., 1997.

Hyde, Margaret O. *Missing and Murdered Children*. New York: Franklin Watts, 1998.

Hyde, Margaret O., and Elizabeth H. Forsyth, M.D. *The Sexual Abuse of Children and Adolescents*. Brookfield, Conn.: The Millbrook Press, Inc., 1997.

Internet Addresses

ChildAbuse.com

<http://www.childabuse.com>

> The site features pages of information on topics ranging from the prevention of child abuse to resources to legislation to trends in child abuse.

The Jacob Wetterling Foundation

<http://www.jwf.org>

> The site offers information about laws that protect children as well as safety tips for kids.

The KlaasKids Foundation

<http://www.klaaskids.org>

> Statistics on the number of sex offenders registered by state can be found at the site.

The National Center for Missing and Exploited Children

<http://www.missingkids.com>

This site features photographs and data about missing children, as well as safety tips, statistics, and the organization's history.

Parents for Megan's Law

<http://www.parentsformeganslaw.com>

This site offers tips on protecting children from sex offenders and links to sex offender registries nationwide, as well as insight and information on Megan's Law notifications.

The Polly Klaas Foundation

<http://www.pollyklaas.org>

This site includes tips on ways neighbors can keep an eye on their community, as well as information about Polly Klaas and how the foundation works to help prevent crimes against children.

For More Information

Prominent foundations named after murdered or missing children can be contacted as follows:

Adam Walsh Children's Fund
9176 Alternate A1A, Suite 200
Lake Park, FL 33403–1452
telephone: (561) 863–7900
fax: (561) 863–3111
e-mail: awcf@ncmec.org

The Jacob Wetterling Foundation
P.O. Box 639
St. Joseph, MN 56374
telephone: (320) 363–0470 or (800) 325–HOPE
fax: (320) 363–0473
Web site: <http://www.jwf.org>

Joan Angela D'Alessandro Memorial Foundation
P.O. Box 336
Hillsdale, NJ 07642

KlaasKids Foundation
P.O. Box 925
Sausalito, CA 94966
telephone: (415) 331–6867
fax: (415) 331–5633
e-mail: klaaskids@pacbell.net
Web site: <http://www.klaaskids.org>

Megan Nicole Kanka Foundation
P.O. Box 9956
Trenton, NJ 08650
telephone: (609) 890–2201
fax: (609) 890-2541

The Polly Klaas Foundation
P.O. Box 800
Petaluma, CA 94953
telephone: (800) 587–4357
e-mail: pklaasfdtn@aol.com
Web site: <http://www.pollyklaas.org>

Index